TO TRAIN UP A KNIGHT

TRAINING SONS TO SERVE KING & KINGDOM

JEREMY SPROUSE

KAIO PUBLICATIONS, INC.

To Train Up a Knight: Training Sons to Serve King and Kingdom
Copyright © 2016 by Jeremy Sprouse
Published by Kaio Publications

All rights reserved. No part of this publication may be reproduced, stored in a retrieval system, or transmitted in any form by any means, electronic, mechanical, photocopy, recording, or otherwise, without the prior permission of the author, except as provided for by USA copyright law.

Cover design & book layout: Ben Giselbach
First printing 2016
Printed in the United States of America

Scripture taken from the New King James Version, unless otherwise indicated.
Copyright © 1982 by Thomas Nelson, Inc. Used by permission. All rights reserved.

ISBN: 978-099604306-9

Dedication:

This book is dedicated to Jaden, Isaiah, Isaac, Ean, and Joseph — my knights in training.

"Be on the alert, stand firm in the faith, act like men, be strong."
~1 Corinthians 16:13

TABLE OF CONTENTS

Introduction .... *iii*

Lesson 1: YOUR TRAINING BEGINS *1*
Lesson 2: THE POOR IN SPIRIT *5*
Lesson 3: THOSE WHO MOURN *7*
Lesson 4: THE MEEK *11*
Lesson 5: THE HUNGRY AND THIRSTY *15*
Lesson 6: THE MERCIFUL *17*
Lesson 7: THE PURE *21*
Lesson 8: THE PEACEMAKERS *25*
Lesson 9: THE PERSECUTED *29*

"THE BLESSINGS OF SERVICE" CEREMONY *31*

Lesson 10: THE CHALLENGE OF CHIVALRY *35*
Lesson 11: STARTING WITH FAITH *39*
Lesson 12: SUPPLYING VIRTUE *43*
Lesson 13: SUPPLYING KNOWLEDGE *47*
Lesson 14: SUPPLYING SELF-CONTROL *51*
Lesson 15: SUPPLYING PERSEVERANCE *55*
Lesson 16: SUPPLYING GODLINESS *59*
Lesson 17: SUPPLYING BROTHERLY KINDNESS *63*
Lesson 18: SUPPLYING LOVE *65*

"THE JOURNEY OF CHIVALRY" CEREMONY *69*

Lesson 19: THE ARMOR OF GOD *73*
Lesson 20: THE BELT OF TRUTH *77*
Lesson 21: THE BREASTPLATE OF RIGHTEOUSNESS *81*

TO TRAIN UP A KNIGHT

Lesson 22: FEET PREPARED BY THE GOSPEL.................................. *85*
Lesson 23: THE SHIELD OF FAITH... *89*
Lesson 24: THE HELMET OF SALVATION *93*
Lesson 25: THE SWORD OF THE SPIRIT....................................... *97*
Lesson 26: THE PRAYERS OF THE SAINTS.................................. *101*

"THE ARMOR OF GOD" CEREMONY..*105*

Introduction

KNIGHTS are considered by many to be the pinnacle of honor and virtue, noble men who helped others and fought with courage and bravery. They are known as men who served their lord loyally and faithfully. Even the term *knight* itself comes from the Old English word *cniht*, which means "servant."[1] Such men, however, do not happen by accident—they are the result of training. In ancient times, a knight would begin his training at the age of six or seven. He would be sent to a nearby castle to begin his education and training by serving as what they called a "page." As a page, he would learn horseback riding, archery, wrestling, and would play with wooden swords. These pursuits, however, would not be the emphasis of a page's training. At this stage in a future knight's training, it is more important for him to learn how to interact with authority and to treat others with respect.

Pages would be taught to pay the utmost respect to their trainers and their king, to reverence such men as they would their father, and to behave with humility and meekness. They would be required to serve at meals and keep cups full. Some pages would be given a book on manners called *The Babees' Book*. Notice a brief excerpt from this book:

> Look you be true in word and deed, the better shall you prosper; for truth never works a man shame, but rather keeps him out of sin. The ways to Heaven are twain, mercy and truth, say clerks; and he who will come to the life of bliss must not fail to walk therein.
>
> Make no promise save it be good, and then keep it with all your might, for every promise is a debt that must not be remitted through falsehood.

---

1 Soanes, Catherine, and Angus Stevenson, eds. *Concise Oxford English Dictionary* (Oxford, UK: Oxford University Press, 2004) n. pag.

> Love God and your neighbor, and thus may ye say without fear or dread that you keep all the law.
>
> Uncalled go to no council, scorn not the poor, nor hurt any man, learn of him that can teach you, be no flatterer or scoffer, oppress not your servants, be nor proud, but meek and gentle, and always walk behind your betters.
>
> When your better shows his will, be silent; and in speaking to any man keep our hands and feet quiet, and look up into his face, and be always courteous.[2]

These instructions regarding manners, conduct, and service are at the core of a page's training. It is this core that the devotionals in this book strive to teach (while maybe using some of the combat activities just for fun).

The devotionals in this book are aimed at boys between the ages of 6 and 12. Just as pages were primarily instructed by a strong male figure, these devotionals are intended for fathers to do with their son(s). Of course, they can be used in other ways such as in family devotionals and by single moms. If at all possible, however, it should be the father. Fathers have been given the responsibility to train and instruct their children in God's ways (cf. Ephesians 6:4, Deuteronomy 6:1-9). We must take this responsibility seriously. It is not a responsibility fathers can hand off to the mothers, a Sunday school teacher, a youth minister, or anyone else. Fathers must be actively engaged in the training of their children and especially their sons. They need a strong male figure to show them how to serve the Lord. The devotionals in this book will help guide and instruct, but it is a father's example and the time he spends with his son(s) that will make the difference. This will take time and effort, but there is a rich reward as well. God knows what He is talking about, and the bond

---

[2] Rickert, Edith and L. J. Taylor, trans., *The Babees Book: Medieval Manners for the Young* (Cambridge, Ontario: In parentheses Publications, 2000) http://www.yorku.ca/inpar/babees_rickert.pdf 24 Aug. 2016.

INTRODUCTION

between a father and son is never stronger than when they spend time together studying and applying God's Word.

The devotionals will be most effective with proper preparation. Read through the lesson and all of the Scripture references before sitting down with your son. Apart from the first devotional in each unit, each devotional will have four parts:

- Lesson—a description of a principle of godly living.
- Champion—a Bible character that displays the principle.
- Strategy—questions and discussion to put the principle into action.
- Quest—an activity that either reinforces the principle or provides an opportunity for fun (these usually require a little preparation).

The devotionals are intended primarily as jumping-off points—details, stories, and examples from your life and theirs will make the devotionals a richer and more useful experience. Talk about and explain the Scriptures referenced but not discussed in the devotional. Don't be in too much of a rush to get through these lessons, but don't have months between each lesson either. I would recommend going through no more than one a week, and no fewer than one a month. Most importantly, pray. Pray as you prepare, pray as you begin a devotional, and pray as you end a devotional.

TO TRAIN UP A KNIGHT

LESSON 1

Your Training Begins

IF you were to think about becoming a knight, you would probably think about strapping armor on, taking up a sword, and entering into a great battle. The ideal knight, however, would have been much more than a mere warrior. They would be brave and courageous, but they are also humble and good men who helped others and served their king with honor. The ideal knight is still needed today—men who will dedicate their lives to serving the King and His Kingdom. Jesus instructed us to "seek first the Kingdom of God and His righteousness, and all these things shall be added to you" (Matthew 6:33). We need to learn to serve in God's Kingdom by making our service to God and His Kingdom the first and foremost goal of our lives. To do this, we have to take up the righteous lifestyle that pleases God.

Even in the time of the knights, they recognized there were more than physical battles to fight—there was a spiritual battle (cf. Ephesians 6:10-13). To fight this battle, they knew they had to arm themselves with the ways of God. The image on the next page from a 13th-century manuscript shows a depiction of a knight in this spiritual battle.

This picture is a little different from the ones we are used to seeing (and the words are all in Latin), so let me describe it a little to you. On the left side, we have the enemy. They are snarling, evil-looking monsters that represent the sins and wickedness of man: pride, anger, laziness, insults, discord, stealing, etc. (Note: the illustration has big monsters and little monsters. This represents a distinction men sometimes make between big sins and little sins, but the Bible makes no such distinction.) On the right side, we have the knight armed for battle with his shield of faith (on it is written: The Father, the Son, and the Holy Spirit). Before him are seven gifts from the Holy Spirit taken from Isaiah 11:2-3 (the fear of God, piety, knowledge, fortitude, counsel, intelligence, and understanding) and seven virtues taken from Matthew 5:3-9 (poor in spirit, mourning, meekness, righteousness, mercy, purity, and peace). Above him is an angel with scrolls coming from it describing the blessings of what we call the Beatitudes (Matthew 5:3-12).

While people do not battle with swords in shining armor today, the fight against these sins is still raging. Like the knights of old, we need to take up armor and weapons, but we need to take up the armor and weapons of our Lord. "For though we walk in the flesh, we do not war according to the flesh. For the weapons of our warfare are not carnal but mighty in God for pulling down strongholds" (2 Corinthians 10:3-4). To do this, we are going to learn about the service and attitudes of a knight, the weapons, and the armor that will defend us in our battle. If we are going to overcome the enemy and serve our King with honor and courage, we must learn to live the kind of life that pleases God.

YOUR TRAINING BEGINS

If you are ready to begin your training, sign your name to the contract on page 5. Then, read it and shout "For the King and His Kingdom" as loud as you can.

DAILY DRILLS:

Aim at reviewing the blessings of Matthew 5:3-10 with your son(s) once at day (maybe at night as they are going to bed). The first night, just do "the poor in spirit." When they can complete it from memory, the next night, add "those who mourn" until they can do both from memory and so on until they can complete all eight blessings from memory.

>Father: "Blessed are the poor in spirit..."

>Son(s): "For theirs is the Kingdom of Heaven."

>Father: "Blessed are those who mourn..."

>Son(s): "For they shall be comforted."

>Father: "Blessed are the meek..."

>Son(s): "For they shall inherit the earth."

>Father: "Blessed are those who hunger and thirst for righteousness..."

>Son(s): "For they shall be filled."

>Father: "Blessed are the merciful..."

>Son(s): "For they shall receive mercy."

>Father: "Blessed are the pure in heart..."

Son(s): "For they shall see God."

Father: "Blessed are the peacemakers…"

Son(s): "For they shall be called sons of God."

Father: "Blessed are those who are persecuted for righteousness' sake…"

Son(s): "For theirs is the Kingdom of Heaven."

After the drill, sing "Seek Ye First."

YOUR TRAINING BEGINS

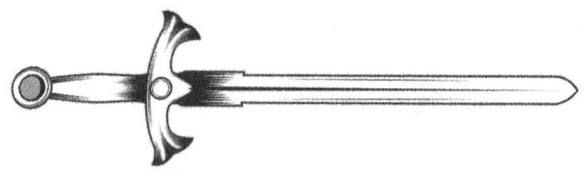

I, _____, agree to begin my training in which I will learn to serve God as my King and to seek the Kingdom of God and His righteousness. I agree to listen respectfully to the lessons from God's Word taught by my father and will do my best to learn how to live a life that pleases God.

Signed: _____
Date: _____

For the King and His Kingdom!

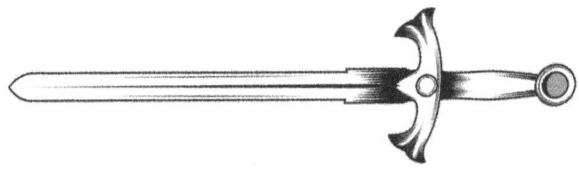

TO TRAIN UP A KNIGHT

LESSON 2

The Poor in Spirit

INSTRUCTION

A knight must be humble. Jesus begins His famous Sermon on the Mount with a series of short statements that show the character and attitudes that please God. The first of these emphasizes humility: "Blessed are the poor in spirit, for theirs is the Kingdom of Heaven" (Matthew 5:3). This does not refer to the amount of money that we have. Instead, it has to do with our attitude towards God and others. If we are poor in spirit, we will not view ourselves as better than others. Being poor in spirit means we recognize that we need God's help as opposed to those who are proud and don't recognize their need for help. If we recognize our spiritual poverty, we will gladly serve Jesus as our Lord and King and only then will we be fit for the Kingdom of Heaven.

Humility not only puts us in the right frame of mind to serve God, but it also puts us in the right frame of mind to serve others. A knight's code often involved protecting the weak. No one, however, protects what he does not value. A man who thinks he is better or more important than others cannot uphold this knightly virtue. Those who view others as less than themselves don't feel the need to share with others; they feel they have the right and might to have what they want, and what others want is of no concern. Those who view others as less than themselves often look at others with contempt and will even mock others and call them names. We may have confidence in our abilities, but the things we know, tasks we do well, or the things we have shouldn't cause us to pridefully put ourselves above others in our hearts and minds. If we want to truly serve God, we need to value others and avoid such cruel actions.

CHAMPION OF HUMILITY

Our champion of humility is a man that as far as we know never even met Jesus, but he has complete faith in Jesus' power to heal. In Luke 7:1-10, a centurion sends a message to Jesus asking for his servant to be healed. Centurions were officers in the Roman army that were given command of one hundred soldiers. As one in authority, this centurion recognizes that Jesus has an even greater authority. Others feel this centurion is a worthy man, but he does not feel worthy—not even worthy enough to come to Jesus personally or to have Jesus under the roof of his house. We also see this man's humility in his care and respect for his servants. Many in his position would not have cared about the life and suffering of their servants, but he does. He is poor in spirit, and Jesus praises him for it (cf. 7:9).

STRATEGY

- Do you consider yourself poor in spirit? Why or why not?
- What actions should a humble person avoid?
- What should a humble person do?
- How do we show that we depend on God?

QUEST: A HUMBLE RACE

Make an obstacle course requiring one to stoop and crawl to get through it (perhaps out of cardboard boxes or under and through chairs). The point? By humbling ourselves we can reach the goal of being with God in Heaven.

LESSON 3

Those Who Mourn

INSTRUCTION

MANY say only the weak cry. They say things like: "Shake it off," "Only babies cry," or "Big boys don't cry." If one is throwing a tantrum or not seriously injured, these sayings may be true, but there are times in our lives where we need to feel a deep sorrow. Jesus emphasizes the second attitude that pleases God is our care and our concern about the ways of God: "Blessed are those who mourn, for they shall be comforted" (Matthew 5:4). To serve God and His Kingdom, we must genuinely care about the ways of God. The sorrow we show when we fall short reflects this care. If it's not a big deal to tell a lie, we don't really care about the ways of God. If seeing the pain and suffering in this world caused by sin doesn't bother us, we do not really care about the ways of God. When we sorrow over our sins in this way, we won't want to repeat them, and it will help us to be better servants (cf. 2 Corinthians 7:9-11). Many comfort themselves by making excuses for what they have done, but real comfort will only come from God when we learn to mourn over sin.

Like humility, this ability to mourn will also put us in the right frame of mind to treat others with respect and kindness. Mistakes happen. We will say words that hurt others. We might even strike out at another or accidentally step on someone's toes. When we have hurt another, whether by words or by actions, whether on purpose or by accident, we need to be able to offer a heartfelt apology. Just being sorry for being caught or apologizing because you have been forced to apologize is not enough. If we are truly sorry, we will apologize as soon as we realize what we have done and will do our best to comfort and make amends to those we have hurt. That is what it means to repent.

CHAMPION OF REPENTANCE

Our champion of repentance is a slave named Onesimus. He seemingly stole money from his master Philemon and ran away. The details of Onesimus' story are uncertain, but we can piece most of it together from Paul's letter to Philemon in verses 10-20. Some time after he runs away, Onesimus meets Paul and becomes a Christian through obedience to the Gospel. He shows true repentance by returning to his master. He does this despite the possibility of great humiliation, pain, and possibly even death. At this time in history, a runaway slave might be whipped or beaten until he is a cripple; he might be branded on his head or arms; the skin under his feet might be burned off by glowing iron plates; a metallic collar with his name and address might be fixed around his throat; he might even be killed as a warning to fellow slaves. He would be completely at the mercy of his master.[1] Fortunately for Onesimus, he has two things going for him that must have been encouraging. First, his master Philemon is a Christian. Second, Paul writes this letter to Philemon urging him to accept Onesimus back as a brother, and we have every reason to believe that is exactly what Philemon does.

STRATEGY

- Why do we make excuses when we know we have done something wrong?
- Do excuses really help us? Why not?
- How do we show we are truly sorry?

    1. Mourn

---

[1] Barth, Markus, and Helmut Blanke, *The Letter to Philemon: A New Translation with Notes and Commentary* (Grand Rapids, MI: Wm. B. Eerdmans Publishing, 2000) 30.

THOSE WHO MOURN

2. Apologize
3. Make amends
4. Change

QUEST: THE CIRCLE OF REPENTANCE

Make a large circle on a paper plate and divide it into four sections. Label the sections: 1) Mourn, 2) Apologize, 3) Make amends, 4) Change. Have your son pick one of the following situations or write them on 3 x 5 index cards and have him draw:
You were loud and distracting during worship services.

- You hit your brother because he wouldn't let you play with his toy.
- You lied to your mom about finishing your chores when you hadn't.
- You took something that didn't belong to you (from a brother, a friend, a store, your mom, or your dad).
- You yelled at your brother because he wouldn't play with you.
- You said something mean to a friend.
- You promised to clean the table but ran outside to play.
- You giggled through prayer/devotional time.
- You played in your room even though you knew you were supposed to be going to sleep.

After he has a situation, have your son toss a coin or small rock into the circle. If it lands in:

- Mourn—he must say what he did wrong, why it was wrong, and how it hurt others.

- Apologize—he must pretend he is addressing the person he has wronged and apologize and ask for forgiveness (remind him he has also wronged God).

- Make amends—he explains how he can try to make the situation right (some situations can't be made right).

- Change—he explains how he can avoid the situation or handle it differently in the future.

Continue playing until you don't want to anymore.

LESSON 4

The Meek

INSTRUCTION

MANY people live according to the iron rule of morality—might makes right. They think being able to do something gives you the right to do it. A knight who wants to serve God, however, will learn to be gentle and kind. Jesus said: "Blessed are the meek, for they shall inherit the earth" (Matthew 5:5). What Jesus is saying has nothing to do with weakness, but rather power that is brought under control. *Nelson's Bible Dictionary* defines *meekness* as "an attitude of humility toward God and gentleness toward men, springing from a recognition that God is in control. Although weakness and meekness may look similar, they are not the same. Weakness is due to negative circumstances, such as lack of strength or lack of courage. But meekness is due to a person's conscious choice. It is strength and courage under control, coupled with kindness."[1]

We find God's approval in meekness. God's greatest servants have been meek. Moses was more humble than all men who were on the face of the earth (Numbers 12:3). Paul urged others by the meekness and gentleness of Christ (2 Corinthians 10:1). To be knights in service to God and Kingdom, it is not only what we do that is important, but what we don't do. We don't run over people, we don't put our needs first, we don't use our strength, brains, knowledge, or skills to assert ourselves or harm others. Instead, we bring our strength under control and couple them with kindness to help others.

---
1 Youngblood, Ronald F., F. F. Bruce, and R. K. Harrison eds., *Nelson's New Illustrated Bible Dictionary* (Nashville, TN: Thomas Nelson Publishers, 1995) n. pag.

TO TRAIN UP A KNIGHT

CHAMPION OF GENTLENESS

Our champion of gentleness is best known for defeating Goliath with a sling and five smooth stones. David is a mighty warrior, but he displays great gentleness as well. David plays a harp to soothe King Saul (1 Samuel 16:14-23). After Saul grows jealous of David and tries to destroy him, David spares Saul's life on two occasions. The first time is in 1 Samuel 24:1-22. Here, Saul has been pursuing David to kill him, and Saul happens to go into a cave where David is hiding. David is just a few feet from his enemy and could easily reach out and kill Saul, but he does not do so because Saul is the Lord's anointed (1 Samuel 24:6). Instead, David cuts the corner off Saul's robe. After Saul leaves the cave, David calls out to him and shows the piece of robe to prove he could have killed Saul but did not. Because of this, the two are reconciled for a time. The second time David spares Saul is in 1 Samuel 26:5-25. This time, David sneaks into Saul's camp and takes his spear and water jug. Again, David tells Saul about this and Saul says: "I have sinned. Return, my son David, for I will not harm you again because my life was precious in your sight this day. Behold, I have played the fool and have committed a serious error" (NASB). David chooses the path of faith and gentleness instead of violence and revenge; this is probably one of many reasons why he is known as a man after God's own heart (cf. Acts 13:22).

STRATEGY

- How do we sometimes act selfishly and try to get our way?
- How can we act with gentleness instead?
- How can you use your skills and knowledge to help others?

QUEST: A SOFT TOUCH

Play a game like Jenga or Pick Up Sticks that requires a soft touch. Build the tower and knock it over. What does strength accomplish? It destroys. Now, build the tower again and use a gentle touch to remove the blocks and build the tower higher. With gentleness, we can build up. God wants us to use gentleness to build others up. See how high you can build the tower. (If you don't have Jenga, you might try stacking dominoes or blocks, or adapt any other game that requires a soft touch.)

TO TRAIN UP A KNIGHT

LESSON 5

The Hungry and Thirsty

INSTRUCTION

EVERYONE has hunger and thirst to do something or get something. Whatever we hunger and thirst after will determine the direction and course of our lives. Not every course we choose in life, however, will be satisfying. In fact, there is only one type of hunger and thirst that is truly satisfying. In Matthew 5:6, Jesus says: "Blessed are those who hunger and thirst for righteousness, for they shall be filled." In this verse, *righteousness* means to do God's will and what pleases Him. To know righteousness, we have to study God's will—His Word. Righteousness must become more than something we just read about; it must become something we do and are! Anyone who wants to serve God needs to hunger and thirst for righteousness (cf. Matthew 6:33).

A person who does not grow thirsty or hungry is either sick or dead! So a person who does not hunger or thirst for righteousness is either spiritually sick or spiritually dead. Many are not getting good spiritual food because they are hungering for other things than righteousness. They may be seeking a new toy, money, to watch T.V., or to be liked by others. These things are not always bad, but they are more like dessert. They are fun for the moment, but they will never really satisfy us. To have a good spiritual diet, we need to eat the main course—righteousness—first. We need to be seeking to study and obey God's Word, to spend time in prayer, to sing songs of praise, and to encourage and help others. These are actions that please God and will truly satisfy us.

TO TRAIN UP A KNIGHT

CHAMPION OF SEEKING

Our champion of seeking is another centurion named Cornelius. We read of his hunger for righteousness in Acts 10:1-6. He is known for his devotion and his fear of God. He is generous towards the poor and prays continually. As a result, he has earned a good reputation among men (cf. Acts 10:22). Even better, however, is the satisfaction he receives from seeking after righteousness. God hears his prayers and sends Peter to teach him about salvation. Cornelius and his household become the first of many Christians who were Gentiles.

STRATEGY

- Name some things people look for in life (e.g., money, fame, cars) and consider if they are righteous or unrighteous.

- What ways do you personally seek righteousness in your life?

- What other ways could you seek righteousness?

QUEST: THE FEAST OF RIGHTEOUSNESS

Take your son(s) out to dinner or prepare one. It doesn't need to be fancy, but try to have some of the followings elements: milk to represent the purity of God's Word (1 Peter 2:2), bread to represent the need to be spiritually nourished daily (John 6:33-35; 1 Timothy 4:6), meat to represent the need to grow and mature (Hebrews 5:12-14), salt and a candle to represent our influence (Matthew 5:13-16), something sweet to represent the satisfaction of serving God (John 10:10).

LESSON 6

The Merciful

INSTRUCTION

A knight must learn to see the needs of others and help them. Many have become so self-centered and selfish they no longer care about the suffering and struggles of others (cf. Matthew 9:11-13; 12:1-7). They are always asking "What's in it for me?" and rarely, if ever, will do something for another if it does not benefit them personally (cf. Matthew 6:1-2). If we act in such uncaring ways, however, we will find no compassion ourselves. Jesus said: "Blessed are the merciful, for they shall obtain mercy" (Matthew 5:7). Mercy is giving or doing something for another at no cost to the one who received it. It is directly connected with love and forgiveness (cf. Matthew 6:12, 14-15). It is the ability to see a need and do something about it (cf. Mathew 9:35–10:1). Mercy is important to God, and we must learn to be merciful if we are going to serve our King and the Kingdom (cf. Matthew 23:23-24).

In ancient times, knights would be given the responsibility of protecting and caring for the people of their land. If we would be like them, we must learn to show mercy. When someone is in need, we must do more than give him empty words of comfort, we must seek to help him (James 2:15-16). We must learn to be kind and compassionate even to our enemies (Romans 12:17-21). If someone wrongs us and asks for forgiveness, we must forgive him (cf. Matthew 18:22-35), not because he deserves forgiveness or kindness, but because of who we are and who we serve. Mercy requires strength of mind and strength of character, but it is worth the effort because by acting mercifully we will receive mercy from God.

CHAMPION OF MERCY

David returns again as our champion of mercy. David is a man who actively searches for others to show kindness. One example of this is his search for a descendant of Saul (2 Samuel 9:1-13). While no one would have expected David to show kindness to the house of his enemy, David holds himself to a higher standard (in part because of his friendship with Jonathan, Saul's son). He finds out about Mephibosheth (Saul's grandson) and gives him all of Saul's lands and invites Mephibosheth to eat at his table frequently. Later David also seeks to show kindness when a foreign king passes away. David reaches out to comfort and console the new king (2 Samuel 10:1-2). David is not one who just sits around and would only help others if they come to him; he is looking for opportunities to show kindness.

We know David also receives great mercy from God. David makes several mistakes, such as moving the Ark of the Covenant incorrectly, which results in Uzzah's death, and even ordering Uriah's death. Despite these errors, God does not remove David from the throne and even gives the throne to David's descendants. Also, He allows David's descendants to build a house for God's name (cf. 2 Samuel 7:7-16). As one who shows mercy, David receives mercy just as the beatitude in Matthew 5:7 promises.

STRATEGY

- Do you think of yourself as a merciful person? Why or why not?
- How can we keep ourselves from becoming self-centered?
- What are ways we can show kindness to others?

QUEST: THE KINDNESS CONTEST

Pick a day and try to outdo each other in performing acts of kindness towards others. One point is awarded for such acts as opening a door for someone, letting someone go in front of you in line, giving up your seat so another can sit, etc. Before beginning, choose an act of kindness that will be done for the winner as a reward.

TO TRAIN UP A KNIGHT

LESSON 7

The Pure

INSTRUCTION

MEN often have a great desire to good and noble deeds. Unfortunately, the hearts of such men become corrupt and they forget the good they planned and do evil and harm instead. We must realize it does not matter how much strength, how much knowledge, or how many skills we possess. If our hearts are corrupt, we will never hear the King say: "Well done, My good and faithful servant." In Matthew 5:8, Jesus said: "Blessed are the pure in heart, for they shall see God." *Pure* means to be clean and holy. Many strive to look pure, but their minds are full of hatred, anger, envy, and bitterness. God, however, wants us to be sincere and genuine, not just putting on a good show. He requires us to be pure in our hearts—not our literal hearts, but our hearts in the sense of who we are and how we think and feel. What is in our hearts will sooner or later come out in our actions (cf. Mark 7:18-23). If we truly want to serve our King and be in His presence, we will strive to have pure hearts (cf. Hebrews 12:14; 1 John 3:2-3).

To be pure in our hearts, we must guard our hearts (cf. Proverbs 4:23). We have to consider what we see and hear (cf. Proverbs 4:20-27) and strive to avoid wicked influences (cf. Psalm 101:3). We cannot let anger dwell in our hearts regardless of what others have done to us. Instead, we must be quick to forgive and forget. We need to learn to be content and thankful for what we have rather than letting our hearts be filled with greed and jealousy. Anger, jealousy, greed, shame, and lust will corrupt our hearts and corrupt our ways. However, if we strive to rid our hearts of these evil influences and think about what is good, our King will give us peace and be with us

TO TRAIN UP A KNIGHT

(cf. Philippians 4:6-9).

CHAMPION OF PURITY

Daniel is one who was taken away from his family and country as a youth and put in a strange country full of false worship and impurity (Daniel 1:1-7). When impure food and wine are set before him, he makes a firm decision not to defile himself, and with great courage and faith does what is necessary to keep his decision (Daniel 1:8-16). Considering his circumstances and surroundings, many would not have considered eating this food to be a big deal. Daniel, however, is observant and determines to guard his heart. He probably knows that once you make a small compromise, it is easier to make a larger compromise. As a result, he refuses to let his surroundings influence him or determine how he would act and think. In fact, Daniel influences his friends and helps them to maintain their purity. As a result, Daniel is greatly rewarded (Daniel 1:17-20), and his actions would frequently bring glory to God (cf. Daniel 2:46-48; 6:25-28). Like Daniel, we need to make up our minds not to let anything defile our hearts. It will take courage and faith, but the rewards are worth it.

STRATEGY

- How is your heart? Sad? Bitter? Angry? Happy? Content?
- Has anyone hurt you or broken a promise?
- Are you worried about anything?
- Are you watching or listening to anything that is wicked?
- Is there anything you need to confess?

QUEST: THE MARK OF SIN

Get a piece of paper, a pencil, an eraser, and a magnifying glass. The piece of paper represents our hearts. At the beginning, the paper is white and smooth just as our hearts start off pure and innocent. Now, write or have your son write the words *anger, hate, pride, lust, jealousy, envy,* and *lying* in large letters across the paper then have your son erase them. Just as writing these words is a lot easier than erasing them, it is easier to let them into our hearts than to get them out of our hearts. Examine the paper with the magnifying glass. No matter how well these words have been erased, there will be traces of the lead left behind, or an imprint of the words, or the paper will be rough where the words were erased. Sin and wickedness will leave a mark on our hearts as well. We cannot fool ourselves into thinking we can engage in wickedness and maintain our purity.

LESSON 8

The Peacemakers

INSTRUCTION

TRUE bravery isn't shown by fighting; any fool can fight (cf. Proverbs 20:3). True bravery is shown by doing something that only a few even try—making peace. Peace is difficult. Even with those we love, we sometimes get into fights. We are often annoyed, irritated, and frustrated with others. If we are not careful, we could spend all of our time fighting. Thus, we need to strive for peace, and in doing so, we will become like our King. In Matthew 5:9, Jesus said: "Blessed are the peacemakers, for they shall be called sons of God." God is a God of peace (1 Thessalonians 5:23) and hates when men destroy peace (Proverbs 6:19). As much as He hates the destruction of peace, though, He loves those who want to make peace. If we are to put our King first and serve Him, we must seek to be peacemakers.

Making peace requires effort. It is an action, not an accident that is just going to happen. It is always made by someone. We become peacemakers by first striving to be peaceful ourselves (cf. Romans 12:17). We treat others with respect and kindness, we curb our tongues, and we strive not to be easily offended. We are polite and use our manners. We treat others the way we want to be treated (Matthew 7:12). When wronged, we may need to simply let the matter go for the cause of peace and unity (1 Corinthians 6:1-8). If a conflict does arise, however, we need to be the ones to take the first step to repair the relationship (Matthew 5:21-26). It takes effort, but being a peacemaker is one of the greatest ways to serve the King and His Kingdom.

CHAMPION OF PEACE

Jacob is our champion of peace. Jacob and his brother Esau have a rocky relationship. From what we know in the Scriptures, Jacob seems to be the main source of the problem. As the younger brother, Jacob desires the birthright and blessing Esau would receive. Esau, on the other hand, doesn't value his birthright and seems more focused on the here and now. Jacob takes advantage of this to get Esau to trade his birthright for a bowl of lentils. What Jacob does to get the blessing, however, is even worse. With his mom's help, he tricks his nearly blind father into thinking he is Esau and receives the blessing that should have been his brother's. Bitterness fills Esau's heart, and he holds a grudge against Jacob (Genesis 27:41). Jacob then flees and twenty years pass before he returns.

Upon Jacob's return, however, he hears that Esau is coming with 400 men. Jacob decides it is time for peace. He first prays to God (Genesis 32:9-12). Then, he sends many and abundant gifts to Esau, which would in part make up for some of what Jacob had stolen from him (Genesis 32:13-20). Also, Jacob pays Esau great respect bowing down to him seven times as he finally comes into his brother's presence (Genesis 33:1-4). There is still some tension, but the brothers are now largely at peace with one another. When their father Isaac dies, they bury him together (Genesis 35:28-29). Making peace is not easy and it often requires sacrifice, but the repaired relationships are worth it.

STRATEGY

- Do you have habits that irritate others and destroy peace?
- What can you do to be more polite and respectful to others?
- Are there grudges you are holding that you need to let go

for the sake of peace?

- How can you restore peace when you have wronged another?

- How could you help others who are fighting make peace with each other?

QUEST: QUENCHING THE FLAMES

Grab a lighter, some paper, and water. Crumble one of the pages and dip it in water and try to light it on fire. Show how it resists the flames. Then, light some of the dry paper and show how easily it burns. Use some water to put it out. When we are disrespectful and easily offended, we are like the dry piece of paper, and fires will easily start in our lives. When we are being polite, willing to overlook offenses, and striving for peace, however, we are like the water—resistant to the flames and able to put them out.

TO TRAIN UP A KNIGHT

LESSON 9

The Persecuted

INSTRUCTION

UNFORTUNATELY, being blessed by God does not mean being blessed by men. We will find many enemies and struggles along the path of righteousness (cf. 2 Timothy 3:12). In Matthew 5:10, Jesus said: "Blessed are those who are persecuted for righteousness' sake, for theirs is the Kingdom of Heaven." Jesus is talking about those who are persecuted for the sake of righteousness—those who will do God's will regardless of any earthly punishment (cf. 1 Peter 2:20). The persecutions Jesus describes are similar to being teased, hit, and lied about (cf. Matthew 5:11). Sometimes it may seem like no one likes us, but we need to realize God does. If we do the will of God and suffer for it, then we will inherit the heavenly Kingdom.

If we are to truly serve our King, we must do what is right regardless of the consequences or the peer pressure we face. This decision needs to be made now before it becomes a hard decision. It is too easy to give in or make excuses if we wait until we are face to face with temptations or enemies. Like Daniel, who purposed in his heart (Daniel 1:8), we must always remember the value and the reward of serving our King—it more than makes up for the trials and insults we will face (cf. Romans 8:18).

CHAMPION OF ENDURING PERSECUTION

Our champion of enduring persecution is the prophet Jeremiah.

He is sometimes called "the Prophet of Doom" or the "the Weeping Prophet." God sends Jeremiah to teach Judah at a time when no one wants to do what is right, and he does not feel up to the task from the start (Jeremiah 1:1-6). He faces many trials. When the king hears just a few lines from a scroll Jeremiah has written, he cuts it up and throws it into the fire (Jeremiah 36:23). At one point, Jeremiah is tossed into a cistern (Jeremiah 38:6). Even worse than these, however, are the daily torments Jeremiah faces. Everyone mocks him and ridicules him daily to the point he sometimes feels like giving up. He tells himself he would not speak anymore in God's name (Jeremiah 20:7-9). His desire to do what is right, however, is stronger than his desire to give up. Jeremiah could not stop speaking God's Word; he says: "His Word was in my heart like a burning fire shut up in my bones; I was weary of holding it back, and I could not" (Jeremiah 20:9). Like Jeremiah, we need to be servants of God who cannot restrain ourselves from doing and speaking what is right.

STRATEGY

- If we follow God, what bad treatment might we receive?

- What can we do to remind ourselves to do right even when everyone else is doing what is wrong?

- Has anyone ever made fun of you for doing what was right? How did it make you feel?

QUEST: THE GREATER REWARD

Get some cookies or small toys. Tell your son if he sits sill and silent for five minutes he can get one; if he sits still and silent for 10 minutes, he can get 2; but if he sits still and silent for 15 minutes, he can have all of them. Waiting and enduring can be difficult, but the reward makes up for the wait.

"The Blessings of Service" Ceremony

CEREMONIES, rituals, and celebrations were a large part of a knight's identity. These things marked his progress towards knighthood. The change from page to squire, helping a knight to don his armor for the first time, receiving his first sword, and such events were all milestones in this journey. This journey ended with a grand ceremony in which a squire was knighted (some of the knighting ceremonies were week-long events). To help show our sons their progress and give them milestones on their journey, we will end each unit with a ceremony and a small gift.

This first ceremony is an opportunity to inspire them and hold them accountable to follow Jesus' teachings in Matthew 5:3-12. How elaborate or large you make this ceremony is, of course, up to you, but consider making this ceremony a rather simple one and only between you and your son(s).

Although small, it should be memorable. A special occasion like a camping trip or even just a bonfire would be a good setting (a sword for the ceremony would be a nice touch as well).

SAMPLE CEREMONY:

In Matthew 5:1-2, Jesus goes up on a mountain and begins teaching the disciples. What follows is one of the greatest and most challenging sermons man has ever heard. It requires us to put aside ourselves and put God first. It requires us to go against our natural reactions and choose God's ways instead. The path may be difficult, like climbing a steep mountain. For those who will trust God and climb the path, however, there are great blessings.

Father: Do you know the blessings of serving the King?

Son(s): Yes!

Father: Kneel and say them with me [Speak the first part of each Beatitude and have your son(s) finish the rest.]

Father: "Blessed are the poor in spirit…"

Son(s): "For theirs is the Kingdom of Heaven."

Father: "Blessed are those who mourn…"

Son(s): "For they shall be comforted."

Father: "Blessed are the meek…"

Son(s): "For they shall inherit the earth."

Father: "Blessed are those who hunger and thirst for righteousness…"

Son(s): "For they shall be filled."

Father: "Blessed are the merciful…"

Son(s): "For they shall receive mercy."

Father: "Blessed are the pure in heart…"

Son(s): "For they shall see God."

Father: "Blessed are the peacemakers…"

Son(s): "For they shall be called sons of God."

Father: "Blessed are those who are persecuted for righteousness sake…"

Son(s): "For theirs is the Kingdom of Heaven."

Father: Always remember the life that pleases God and the

"THE BLESSINGS OF SERVICE" CEREMONY

blessings that come from it. (Son's name), the times we have come together to study these lessons have been a special time for me. I have seen you growing into the kind of man God would have you to be and it makes me proud. I want to give you a small gift to help you remember the lessons you have learned and the kind of life you want to live. [I found necklaces that had a shield on one side and 2 Chronicles 32:8 on the other. JS] (Son's name), I love you.

Before we close, let's make a commitment to follow Jesus' instructions.

All together: For the King and His Kingdom!

> I will be humble.
>
> I will be penitent.
>
> I will be meek.
>
> I will be righteous.
>
> I will be merciful.
>
> I will be pure.
>
> I will be a peacemaker.
>
> I will do right no matter the consequences.

End with a prayer: "Heavenly Father and source of all that is good and wonderful, thank you for the times we have had to study God's Word together and for this occasion in my sons' lives to celebrate their desire to serve You. Help us to seek Your Kingdom and Your righteousness. Let our lives find favor in Your sight. In the name of Jesus, amen."

TO TRAIN UP A KNIGHT

LESSON 10

The Challenge of Chivalry

KNIGHTS would be set apart from other warriors not only by their training and dedication to their king but by what we refer to as a "Code of Chivalry." This so-called "Code of Chivalry" is often talked about as if there were one code of conduct that all knights followed, but in truth, this never existed. Instead, according to Scott Farrell of ChivalryToday.com, "Many people—from successful knights to contemplative philosophers—compiled lists of virtuous qualities, called the 'knightly virtues,' which they felt defined chivalry."[1] The seven most common virtues according to Farrell were courage, justice, mercy, generosity, faith, nobility, and hope. No two lists, however, were ever the same. This is because men often struggle with knowing what is right and wrong. To learn what true chivalry is, we must look beyond the thoughts of men to the thoughts of God (cf. Isaiah 55:8-9). It is only in the Bible that we find a list of qualities that all who would serve the King must strive to have in their lives.

In the Bible and nowhere else we find all things that pertain to life and godliness (2 Peter 1:2-4). The Apostles had walked with Jesus, had seen the way He lived, and had been personally instructed by Jesus. Also, they were reminded of everything Jesus said and were guided into all truth by the Holy Spirit (John 14:25-26; 16:12-15). They had received true knowledge and understanding from Jesus Himself. They passed on that knowledge through their teachings, their writings, and through their examples so that we could have a faith like theirs and rise above the corruption in the world. Not only does this knowledge enable us to escape the corruption of the world, but it also enables us to become partakers of the divine nature—to become more like God. This divine nature is described by eight "Christian graces,"

---
[1] "The Seven Knightly Virtues" http://chivalrytoday.com/knightly-virtues/, 14 Oct. 2015.

or qualities that must be present in our thinking, in our actions, and in our lives if we wish to serve our King: faith, virtue, knowledge, self-control, perseverance, godliness, brotherly kindness, and love (2 Peter 1:5-7). There could be no greater ideals of chivalry than these since they originate from the nature and character of God Himself—they are divine.

We are told to start with faith and then add the other qualities to it. In the Greek language, the word used for *add* or *supply* originally meant "to found and support a chorus, to lead a choir, to keep in tune." It was used of adding voices to a song. In some songs, one person will start off singing by himself, and it is beautiful, but then, another voice is added, and the song begins to fill out and become richer. Then another voice and another are added, until everyone is singing in harmony, working together for a grand overall effect. What started as a beautiful song becomes an incredible and stunning song. These eight qualities are like such a song. Each one of them is important and would be admirable to be found in any individual, but when all of them blend together in one person, then we truly discover the value and the power of Christian chivalry.

Peter goes on to tell us what possessing and increasing in these qualities will do for our lives in 2 Peter 1:8-11. They will help us to be useful in our service to the King (1:8). They will help us see what is really important in life. Without them, it is like we are blind or short-sighted (1:9). We need to remember that our behavior as knights of God needs to be different than the behavior we see in the world; we need to be chivalrous by God's standards. By this, we can gain assurance that we will enter the everlasting Kingdom of our Lord and Savior (1:10-11).

We must recognize, however, that the task before us is not easy. As we look at these qualities, Peter tells us that it will require diligence to add each and every one of them to our lives (2 Peter 1:5). Diligence describes an intense, strenuous effort. Diligence is the tool we use to add all these voices into our lives so they truly sing for our King. While these lessons will teach you about these qualities, it will be up to you to truly add them to your life. You will need to be focused and determined. It will take work and daily effort to achieve them. Are you up to the challenge?

Get a pad of sticky notes and write a Bible verse on several notes. Then, use them to make a trail leading to a treasure that will help them on their quest for chivalry (a Bible, a prayer journal, etc.). Have them follow the trail and read every verse.

DAILY DRILLS:

Aim at reviewing the characteristics of 2 Peter 1:5-7 with your son(s) once a day (maybe at night as they are going to bed).

Father: "With all diligence, to faith…"
Son(s): "Add virtue!"

Father: "With all diligence, to virtue…"
Son(s): "Add knowledge!"

Father: "With all diligence, to knowledge…"
Son(s): "Add self control!"

Father: "With all diligence, to self control…"
Son(s): "Add perseverance!"

Father: "With all diligence, to perseverance…"
Son(s): "Add godliness!"

Father: "With all diligence, to godliness…"
Son(s): "Add brotherly kindness!"

Father: "With all diligence, to brotherly kindness…"
Son(s): "Add love!"

TO TRAIN UP A KNIGHT

After the drill, sing "Soldiers of Christ Arise."

LESSON 11

Starting with Faith

INSTRUCTION

TRUE chivalry begins with faith—the faith that comes from hearing the true knowledge of God. When we know what is true and righteous, we can build our lives on it a firm foundation. It gives us a place from which we can add the other qualities. It gives us the stability we need to keep us serving the King. If we are going to truly serve our King, we must be confident that He is right and true. If we are not firmly convinced of this, we will be filled with doubts about whether or not we are on the right side and might be pulled away from service to our King. It is our faith that can firmly fix us on the right path.

We have to understand that God has given us what we need to know in order to be pleasing to Him and live in His everlasting Kingdom. Remember 2 Peter 1:3 talks of the true knowledge given to the Apostles and through them, given to us. It contains all things about life and godliness. If He has given us all the knowledge we need, there is no more knowledge to receive. Anyone who comes along claiming we need to know something that is not found in the Bible is clearly not teaching God's will. Colossians 2:8 warns us not to be led astray by man's thinking: "Beware lest anyone cheat you through philosophy and empty deceit, according to the tradition of men, according to the basic principles of the world, and not according to Christ." Sometimes what they say may sound reasonable and may even sound better to us, but we must put our faith, our trust, in God and His divine revelation.

TO TRAIN UP A KNIGHT

CHAMPIONS OF FAITH

We have three champions this time, three young men who stand together in faith: Shadrach, Meshach, and Abednego. In Daniel 3, these three young men are given a great test of their faith. Nebuchadnezzar has built a golden statue and demands that everyone worship it or be thrown into a blazing furnace (Daniel 3:1, 4-6). Shadrach, Meshach, and Abednego refuse, and they are brought to Nebuchadnezzar. He gives them one last chance to obey before being tossed into the furnace (Daniel 3:13-15). They say: "O Nebuchadnezzar, we have no need to answer you in this matter. If that is the case, our God whom we serve is able to deliver us from the burning fiery furnace, and He will deliver us from your hand, O king. But if not, let it be known to you, O king, that we do not serve your gods, nor will we worship the gold image which you have set up" (Daniel 3:16-18). They are firmly convinced that their God could deliver them. Even more impressive, though, is they are so convinced their way is right, they believe it is better to stay faithful to God and be burned alive than to compromise their faith. God does deliver them, and they come out of the fire without a mark upon them (Daniel 3:26-27). Even better, King Nebuchadnezzar ends up praising God (Daniel 3:28-29). Shadrach, Meshach, and Abednego know if they stay with God, God would stay with them. Likewise, if we have the faith to stay with Him, He will be with us.

STRATEGY:

- Do you firmly believe God exists? Why or why not?
- Do you have doubts that the Bible is inspired by God? Why or why not?
- Do you believe evolution sounds more reasonable than creation? Why or why not?

- Do you believe there is a Heaven and a Hell? Why or why not?

QUEST: SOLIDIFY

Get some baking clay and one of your son's action figures. Help him roll out the clay and make an imprint with his action figure (if you are having problems with the clay sticking to the figure, try spraying the figure with some cooking spray). Demonstrate that while it looks like the action figure, it isn't permanent—it can be bent and reshaped. Then, make the imprint again and bake it. Afterward, explain how the image is now fixed. This is what faith does in our relationship with God. When we have a firm conviction in His Word, it will help keep us in His ways.

ALTERNATE:

Get some play dough, some plaster of paris, and one of your kid's action figures. Help them roll out the play dough and make an imprint with their action figure (if you are having problems with the play dough sticking to the figure, try spraying the figure with some cooking spray). Demonstrate that while it looks like the action figure, it isn't permanent—it can be bent and reshaped. Then, make the imprint again, but mix up and pour a little bit of plaster into it and let it dry. When it is ready, pull it out and talk about how the image is more like the figure and it is solid. This is what faith does in our relationship with God. When we have a firm conviction in His Word, it will keep us in His ways and help us to imitate Him better.

TO TRAIN UP A KNIGHT

LESSON 12

Supplying Virtue

INSTRUCTION

MOST of the ideals of chivalry that men came up with can be summed up in one word found in 2 Peter 1:5—*virtue*. *Virtue* is a term that refers to achieving excellence in doing what is right and good. It is the knowledge of the right thing to do plus the desire and courage to do it. Peter uses this word a few verses earlier in 1:3 to describe how they are called through the virtue of Christ. Peter has witnessed the morally excellent life of Jesus—how He dealt with others, how He followed the Law, how He lived uprightly and blamelessly. Now, he is encouraging us to live the way Jesus lived. This is where we really want to make our achievements in life; it is the specific field that we should strive to master—being imitators of Christ.

It takes great courage to live such a life of virtue. Specifically, it takes the courage to act on what you know is right. It is one thing to know how Jesus would act, to be firmly convinced that God's ways are right; but it is another thing to actually live out that faith and act upon it. We need the desire and the courage to act on our faith. A faith that does not change the way we live and serve God is worthless and dead (James 2:14-26). Only when our faith truly changes the way we act and respond to others will we have supplied our faith with virtue.

CHAMPION OF MORAL EXCELLENCE

Daniel is our champion of moral excellence. In Daniel 6:1-3, we read that King Darius is planning to put Daniel in charge of the whole kingdom because he has distinguished himself. The life Daniel lives inspires the king to put him into the greatest position of trust and responsibility. Daniel 5:12 notes that Daniel has a reputation for having an extraordinary spirit, knowledge, and understanding. The king's plans, however, disturb his other officials. They begin to search for some fault in Daniel or corrupt deed, but they cannot find anything he has done wrong (Daniel 6:4). They realize the only way they are going to be able to catch Daniel in anything is if they can get the king to pass a law that would make it illegal for Daniel to serve God (Daniel 6:5). So, they trick the king into passing a law saying anyone who prayed to any god or man except the king for thirty days would be thrown into the lions' den (Daniel 6:6-9).

What Daniel does next truly show his moral character. When he finds out about the decree, he ignores it and continues to pray and serve God as he has always done. Now, he could have prayed privately or hidden his service, but he doesn't even try to cover up his prayer life. In Daniel 6:10, he kneels before a publicly visible window three times every day and gives thanks to God. He is telling others through his actions there is no threat that they can make that will stop him from serving God.

As the events unfold, the men clearly see Daniel praying and bring him before the king. Although the king doesn't want to punish Daniel, he is forced by his law to throw Daniel into the lions' den. The next morning, the king checks on Daniel and Daniel says, "My God sent His angel and shut the lions' mouths, so that they have not hurt me, because I was found innocent before Him; and also, O king, I have done no wrong before you" (Daniel 6:22). Notice Daniel lives in such a way that he does no wrong before men, and he knows his salvation comes from being innocent before God. Likewise, if we are to add virtue to our faith, we must diligently work to do no wrong to man and be innocent before God.

STRATEGY

- How can we learn what is morally excellent?
- How can we know what Jesus would do?
- What is something you know you should do, but are afraid to do or have difficulty doing?

QUEST: MORAL COMPASS

Get a compass and a map. Explain how the compass needle always points north and the other directions can be determined. Then, show how the compass helps to orient us on a map. By pointing north, the compass helps us to determine the right direction to go. Each of us needs to have what some call a moral compass—the ability to determine what is right and what is wrong and to act accordingly. As a compass points north, so our moral compass must point towards God. God is the one who determines what is right and wrong, and only through His Word can our moral compass be truly accurate.

LESSON 13

Supplying Knowledge

INSTRUCTION

KNOWLEDGE isn't typically included on most of the man-made codes of chivalry. A true knight of God, however, knows that he doesn't have the knowledge to do what is right in all circumstances. He knows that such information only comes from God's inspired Word. Knowledge has always been important to serving God (cf. Hosea 4:6). So, it's no wonder we find it on the list of qualities a Christian must have to bear fruit and be useful in His Kingdom (cf. 2 Peter 1:8). We are told to be diligent to be workers who can accurately handle God's Word (2 Timothy 2:15)—this can only be accomplished by consistently studying and meditating on God's Word. By diligently studying God's Word, we can get a complete picture of what is a truly right and worthy life. It enables us to conduct ourselves properly in the household of God and support the truth (1 Timothy 3:15). It is through the words of faith that we will receive the nourishment and strength we need to serve God faithfully (1 Timothy 4:6).

We must also recognize that much of our battle as knights of God will be in the realm of knowledge. There is false and deceptive knowledge that is harmful to us and should be rejected (cf. Colossians 2:8; 1 Timothy 1:4; 4:7). In addition, we need to be able to make a defense for the hope we have in Christ (1 Peter 3:15). In 2 Corinthians 10:3-6, Paul describes the knowledge God gives us as a powerful weapon, a weapon that can pull down strongholds by casting down arguments every high thing that exalts itself against the knowledge of God. We can and should take every thought captive to the obedience of Christ.

We must make learning the Bible a focus and priority in our lives. Paying attention to Bible classes and sermons, frequently reading the Scriptures, and memorizing Bible passages will all help with this goal. With all diligence, we must add virtue to our faith, and knowledge to our virtue (2 Peter 1:5).

CHAMPION OF STUDYING

Our champion of studying is a scribe by the name of Ezra. In Ezra 7:10, we find that Ezra has set his heart to accomplish three goals. His first goal is to study the Law of the Lord. This word *study* means "to seek with care."[1] Ezra sets his heart to making careful inquiries of God's law for knowledge, advice, and insight. His second goal is to practice the Law of the Lord. He has not only committed his life to studying the Law, but also to applying it to his life and practicing it. He recognizes that the real value of knowing God's Word comes when we practice it. The third goal is to teach His statutes and ordinances. He recognizes the tremendous value of what he studies and practices and wants others to experience it as well. Ezra 7:9 tells us that God's favor is upon Ezra because of his goals. Likewise, when we set our hearts to study, follow, and teach God's Word, we can find His favor. Then, we will have added knowledge to our faith and virtue.

STRATEGY

- Do you enjoy reading God's Word?
- Are you in the habit of reading God's Word daily?
- Do you understand what you read?
- What Scriptures do you have memorized?

---

[1] Harris, R. Laird, Gleason L. Archer Jr., and Bruce K. Waltke, eds., *Theological Wordbook of the Old Testament* (Chicago, IL: Moody Press,1999) n. pag.

QUEST: A SHARPER EDGE

Get a toy sword, a sharp knife, and some paper. Show how the toy sword doesn't really cut; it just mashes things up and makes a mess. Then, show how the knife cuts the paper easily. Explain how knowledge is like the knife. When we are merely doing what we think is right and important, we are going to make a mess of our lives like the toy sword. When we train ourselves with God's knowledge, however, we become sharp and useful.

TO TRAIN UP A KNIGHT

LESSON 14

Supplying Self-Control

INSTRUCTION

KNIGHTS need to be masters of control. They would need to be able to control their horses, their lances, their swords, and their shields. It would be most important, however, that they are able to control themselves. Self-control is essential to any knight who practices chivalry. Acquiring self-control means rising above the behavior of brute beasts and taking control of ourselves rather than giving in to every desire and being led by our emotions (cf. 2 Peter 2:12). God's Word tells us to control our lusts (1 Thessalonians 4:3-6; 1 Peter 4:1-4), our tongues (James 3:2-12), our bodies (1 Corinthians 6:12-20), and our minds (Colossians 2:8; Philippians 4:8; 2 Corinthians 10:5). The ultimate goal is to exercise self-control in all things (cf. 1 Corinthians 9:25).

To gain self-control, we need to realize it is possible not to give in to temptation. First Corinthians 10:13 tells us God will not allow us to be tempted beyond what we can handle. This means we can endure any temptation put before us. God provides a way of escape so that we can endure temptations. Notice, the way of escape is not always a removal from the temptation; sometimes we have to stand firm against temptations.

There are several tools God has given us to help in this task. The first is prayer (cf. James 5:13-18). It is much easier to resist temptations when you are in the very act of talking with God. Another tool is the Scriptures. In Matthew 4, Jesus quotes Scripture to resist the devil's temptations. Memorizing verses that relate to the temptations we struggle with keeps our minds in the right place. There is a thinking process that goes along with most sins. If we stop it in the mind, we can stop the body from acting (cf. James 1:13-15). Also, it is helpful to find something good to occupy ourselves rather than dwelling on the temptation (cf. Matthew 12:43-45; Ephesians 4:28-32). If we diligently use these tools, we can add self-control to our knowledge, virtue, and faith.

CHAMPION OF CONTROL

Our champion of control is Lot. Lot is best known as Abraham's nephew. He lived in Sodom and Gomorrah—two cities that engage in such perverseness and wickedness that God destroys them with brimstone. Lot, however, doesn't let his surroundings affect his behavior; he lives righteously (2 Peter 2:6-9). It isn't easy for him; these verses describe his oppression by the filthy conduct of others and the daily torment of his soul as he sees and hears what they are doing. God, however, delivers him from all of this and Lot stands as an assurance that "the Lord knows how to deliver the godly out of temptations" (2 Peter 2:9). We need to exercise self-control so that we can be like Lot and live righteously no matter what our surroundings may be.

STRATEGY

- Do you struggle with keeping your emotions under control?
- How can we keep our emotions from controlling us?
- What places or what times do you find yourself the most tempted?
- How have you tried to resist temptations?
- What Scriptures could you memorize to help you?

SUPPLYING SELF-CONTROL

QUEST: TAKE CONTROL

Grab a remote control car and set up an obstacle course. Take turns running the car through the course and explaining how the remote controls the car and helps it to avoid obstacles. Similarly, we need to exercise control over our bodies and emotions so that we will avoid temptations and obstacles to our spiritual lives.

LESSON 15

Supplying Perseverance

INSTRUCTION

CHIVALRY can be tough to practice. It is easy to be kind once, to tell the truth once, or to study your Bible once, but true chivalry requires us to do such things all the time. So, in 2 Peter 1:6, we are told to add perseverance to our self-control. We need to do more than just control ourselves for a moment; our goal is to be in control for a lifetime.

To gain perseverance, we need to be aware of the pitfalls that cause people to give up. Some have no clear purpose or see no real meaning in serving God, and they simply get bored or tired and drift away (cf. Hebrews 2:1-4). Some lose the path because they have listened to false teachings given by man instead of God's Word (cf. Colossians 2:8; Luke 8:5, 12). Some give up because they think it is too difficult (Luke 8:6, 13). They don't have the faith that God's ways are best when faced with trials, or that they can resist temptation and live righteously. Some get distracted by worry or money and what it can buy (Luke 8:7, 14). Also, some give up because they have made a mistake or many mistakes, and they get discouraged and lose hope.

These pitfalls, however, can be overcome. First, we need to learn the Scriptures. Romans 15:4 tells us God's Word is more than just an "instruction book." It is a book that motivates us; it is a book that encourages us and helps us to be better. This helps us avoid false doctrines (cf. 2 Peter 3:15-18). Also, we need to be involved in serving God. In Hebrews 11, we find example after example of what godly men and women do with their faith. Every time their faith leads them to do something. When we are active in service, it helps us endure and keeps us from becoming bogged down with worry and sin (Hebrews 10:32-39; 12:1-4). Last, remember that everyone makes mistakes, but our mistakes don't have to define us. Proverbs 24:16 says, "A righteous man may fall seven times and rise again." It is our ability to rise after falling that will truly define us. We must each take on Paul's attitude and focus: "Forgetting those things which are behind and reaching forward to those things which are ahead, I press toward the goal for the prize of the upward call of God in Christ Jesus" (Philippians 3:13-14). We can persevere as long as we remember the hope and encouragement we have in God and keep striving for the goal.

CHAMPION OF PERSEVERING

Joseph, the son of Jacob, is our champion of persevering. Joseph has a great life that comes to a crashing halt when his jealous brothers toss him into a well and then sell him as a slave (Genesis 37). Instead of stewing in anger or giving up, he serves his master Potiphar as best he can. He ends up becoming overseer of all that Potiphar owns (Genesis 39:2-4). Unfortunately, Potiphar's wife is not a character of moral excellence. She fancies Joseph, but Joseph refuses to have anything to do with her. In Genesis 39:9, he tells her, "How then can I do this great wickedness, and sin against God?" Joseph recognizes that serving God means maintaining a standard of moral excellence. Eventually, Potiphar's wife grabs his clothes, and Joseph has to flee, leaving his clothes behind to maintain his purity (39:10-12). Jealous and angry, Potiphar's wife uses his clothes as "evidence" that Joseph attacked her, and he winds up in jail (39:13-20). Joseph, however, once again lives in such a way that he becomes responsible for everything done in the jail and is even in charge of all the prisoners (39:21-23). Eventually, Joseph interprets Pharaoh's dream and ends up becoming second in command of all of Egypt (41:38-44). Time and again, people recognize there is something admirable about Joseph, they put him in charge of others, and Pharaoh even refers to him having a divine spirit (41:38). Joseph faces injustice and setbacks again and again, but he perseveres, and God helps him rise to the top again and again (cf. Proverbs 24:16). Like Joseph, we will find success if we never give up serving God.

STRATEGY

- Does following the Bible seem too difficult to you?
- Do you ever feel like giving up?
- How do you keep from getting discouraged?
- Why should we have hope?

QUEST: DON'T QUIT

Play the game Operation (or a something similar). The game requires patience and control to remove the diseases from the patient. Some of the pieces are removed easily; others are more difficult. If you make a mistake, it can be frustrating, but there is nothing to do but try again the next time. Keep going until all of the diseases are removed. Explain how perseverance means diligently trying to remove any spiritual sickness in our lives. We will make mistakes, but we can succeed if we keep trying.

TO TRAIN UP A KNIGHT

LESSON 16

Supplying Godliness

INSTRUCTION

THE most chivalrous knight possible would be one who wholeheartedly serves God and treats others with compassion. We call this concept godliness or piety. In essence, godliness is a focus on the two greatest commands (cf. Mark 12:28-31): 1) To love the Lord your God with all your heart, soul, strength, and mind, and 2) To love your neighbor as yourself. It is not only a focus on worshipping God correctly and fulfilling His will but also a focus on treating others as God would treat them. Godliness is something that will bring tremendous value into our lives, both in this world and the one to come (1 Timothy 4:8; 6:6).

We learn to develop godliness through the study of God's Word. In 1 Timothy 6:3-5, Paul explains there is a doctrine (a teaching) that helps us live with godliness. We must reject all other teachings (cf. 1 Timothy 4:6-7). Living a life of godliness needs to be a focus in our prayers as well (cf. 1 Timothy 2:1-4). First Timothy 6:3-5 also gives us some indications that godliness is lacking in our lives: pride, ignorance of God's Word, envy, strife, slander, evil suspicions, and constant fighting. God's Word is that which trains us to see others as God does and treat them accordingly. Such training should remove evil attitudes like envy or jealousy and behaviors that cause unnecessary strife and conflicts with others (cf. Romans 12:18). Remember, all things pertaining to godliness come through the true knowledge of Jesus (2 Peter 1:3). We learn what godliness means by studying the life of Jesus. If we serve God as Jesus did and treat others as Jesus did, our lives will be filled with godliness.

CHAMPION OF GODLINESS

Our champion of godliness is a man by the name of Job. He is a great spiritual man, better than any other living during his time. He is a blameless and upright man who fears God and shuns evil (Job 1:1). He does more than just avoid evil; he leads his family in spiritual matters and worship. He goes to great efforts to keep his children devoted to God and make sure their hearts are pure (Job 1:4-5). He is also one who displays great compassion and kindness towards others (cf. Job 29:11-16). On top of all of this, Job faces more pain and suffering in his life than most ever will—everything he has, all of his family, and even his health are destroyed. Despite this, he stays faithful to God. His life shows us what godliness is all about—focusing on serving God and helping others. His religion truly means something in his life. It isn't just a show; he doesn't do it for glory or to be liked by others. He serves God with his whole heart.

STRATEGY

- Do you feel like you focus on praying and serving God?
- Do you think you serve God with all your heart, soul, strength, and mind?
- How do you think you could be more focused on God in your life?
- Do you feel that you treat others the way Jesus would treat them?
- How could you be more like Jesus in your life?

QUEST: THE PATH OF GODLINESS

Take a road trip! Pick a destination and go. Along the way, explain how you need to go down the right road and follow the laws to reach your destination. In addition, you need to think of others: make sure you don't cut anyone off, and use your turn signals, etc. Likewise, we have a destination—Heaven. To reach that destination, we need to follow the path God has laid out for us and obey His laws. We also need to be watching out for others and helping them along the way.

TO TRAIN UP A KNIGHT

LESSON 17

Supplying Brotherly Kindness

INSTRUCTION

KNIGHTS would frequently band together by purpose and belief. From the legends of Arthur and the Knights of the Round Table to historical orders of knighthood such as the Knights Templars, knights would form communities in which they trained together, stood together, and fought together for their cause. Among such knights there would be such a strong bond that they would do anything for each other. It is important that we also learn to show such brotherly kindness to one another if we are going to reach the ideal lifestyle God has set before us. In 2 Peter 1:7, we are told to add brotherly kindness to our godliness. This is the natural result. If we are focused on serving God and treating others as He would treat them we are naturally going to develop affection for one another.

Brotherly kindness is affection for God's servants that we do not have towards the world (cf. Romans 12:10; Galatians 6:1-2, 10; Hebrews 3:13; 1 Peter 4:8). It is seen in our unity (Ephesians 4:1-3). It is displayed when we help one another (Hebrews 13:1-3). It encourages us to think the best of others (Philippians 2:1-4) and to encourage each other to do good (Hebrews 10:23-25). Only when we live this way will we have added brotherly kindness to the list of qualities that define us.

CHAMPION OF BROTHERLY KINDNESS

Our champion of brotherly kindness is Jonathan, King Saul's son.

TO TRAIN UP A KNIGHT

When David is brought into Saul's household, Jonathan and David become like brothers and best friends. They even make a pact with each other that they would always be friends (1 Samuel 18:1-3). Jonathan shows kindness by giving gifts to David (1 Samuel 18:4), by warning David when Saul is seeking his life (1 Samuel 19:1-3), and by defending David to his father (1 Samuel 19:4-7). He also acts as a spy to find out if David is in danger (1 Samuel 20:1-42). Jonathan knows he won't be the next king of Israel, but that David would be instead. Despite this, he isn't jealous. He expresses his faith that God would establish David as king and encourages him (1 Samuel 20:14-17; 23:16-18). Jonathan and David aren't brothers, but Jonathan treats David as a brother by sharing with him, protecting him, and encouraging him.

STRATEGY

- Do you feel that you are helpful to others?
- What could you do to be more helpful?
- What kind of actions and attitudes discourage others? (e.g., complaining, arguing, selfishness, etc.)
- What can you do to avoid these actions?
- Is there anyone you can think of that could use some encouragement?
- What can you do for them?

QUEST: THE MEAL OF KINDNESS

Help your son(s) prepare a meal for the family as a way of demonstrating kindness. Pre-made foods are fine, but the more involved they can be, the better. Encourage them to choose foods they know others like, set the table, serve the food, and clean up

LESSON 18

Supplying Love

INSTRUCTION

THE last in our list of ideals of chivalry goes above and beyond what men find honorable and worthy. To our brotherly kindness, we add love (2 Peter 1:7). This is not the mushy-gushy kind of romantic love seen in movies, nor is it the kind of love that speaks for a mere fondness for something (e.g., "I love pizza"). It is not even describing the natural love we have for our family. It is above all these kinds of love. It is describing a love that is not based on emotions but on a choice—the choice to seek what is best for others. Agape love is unconditional in that we love others no matter how they treat us. This is the greatest expression of the true knowledge of God (cf. 2 Peter 1:2-3). It is the ultimate expression of God's character (cf. 1 John 4:7-10).

In many ways, this kind of love is the result of many of the concepts we have been studying. It is seen when we are concerned for others and what they are going through (Romans 12:15). When we refuse to think of ourselves as better than others (Romans 12:16-17), we show agape love. It is also seen when we are striving to be at peace with others (Romans 12:18). It is a love that is offered even to our enemies and those who are mistreating us (Matthew 5:43-48; Romans 12:14). It requires a trust in God that He will make everything right and fair (Romans 12:19-21). This is the kind of love that Jesus says would identify those who are truly His disciples (John 13:34-35). It is essential that we diligently aim to add agape love to our brotherly kindness, godliness, perseverance, self-control, knowledge, virtue, and faith. Then we will be truly effective servants in God's Kingdom.

CHAMPION OF LOVING OTHERS

Our champion of loving others is a Levite named Joseph, but we know him better as Barnabas. He is given this name by the Apostles because it means "son of encouragement." There are several events that show us just how fitting this name is to Barnabas. In Acts 4:34-37, Barnabas sells his land and gives it to the Apostles so that no Christian would be in need. His selflessness and kindness must have encouraged many. Later, when the apostle Paul is finding difficulty being accepted in Jerusalem because of his past as a persecutor, Barnabas is the one who speaks up for him and confirms his faith (Acts 9:26-27). He is willing to step in and be a friend to those who have none. We see his encouraging nature again in Acts 15:36-41. This time it is on behalf of his cousin Mark. Mark had started off with Paul and Barnabas on their first missionary journey, but had abandoned them along the way (cf. Acts 13:13). Despite abandoning them, Barnabas is determined to give Mark a second chance even though Mark had wronged them. Paul, however, absolutely refuses. Barnabas ends up taking Mark on a separate journey from Paul's. Later, Paul would acknowledge that Mark is a good worker (cf. Colossians 4:10; 2 Timothy 4:11). Perhaps Mark has changed because of Barnabas' encouragement and willingness to stand up for him. Barnabas is one who sacrifices to help others, he is a friend to the friendless, and he is willing to forgive and let the past go. This is what made him a son of encouragement and such a great example of loving others.

STRATEGY

- Why should we love others?
- How has God loved us?
- Is there anyone you struggle to love?

SUPPLYING LOVE

- What can you do to be more loving?

QUEST: THE FIRES OF LOVE

Make a campfire. Use it to illustrate the ideas of shedding light and warmth to those around. If the campfire were in the open, it could be seen for miles in the darkness. It warms us on a cold night and is useful letting us cook food (e.g., marshmallows). When we love in the way God has commanded, this is the influence we will have on others, and we will be something positive in their lives, something dependable, and something that will show others how God's followers truly behave.

TO TRAIN UP A KNIGHT

The Journey of Chivalry Ceremony

PLAN a long hike for your son(s), one that will be somewhat difficult for them to complete. Get a backpack and gather items to present to them along the way that will remind them of the lessons you have taught them. (Alternatively, you could have a feast and present these items.) Remember, how detailed and complicated you make these ceremonies is up to you; just make it memorable.

SAMPLE CEREMONY

At the start: present them with a walking stick.

> Father: This walking stick represents faith. It is sturdy and dependable. It helps us keep our footing and remove obstacles from our path. There are, however, other qualities of godly chivalry that we need to complete our journey. What is the first quality we need to add to our faith?
>
> Son(s): Virtue
>
> Father: Let's walk.

Stop 1: Present them with a compass.

> Father: This compass represents the need to act and think in ways that show God is in our lives. As it points to north, so we must be examples pointing others towards God. Is our journey complete?
>
> Son(s): No.
>
> Father: What do we need to add to our virtue?

Son(s): Knowledge.

Father: Let's keep going.

Stop 2: Present them with a map.

> Father: This maps represents the need to know God's ways. Maps help us determine our course and evaluate how far we've gone. So the Word of God lays out a path for us and helps us evaluate our spiritual lives. Is our journey complete?

Son(s): No.

Father: What do we need to add to our knowledge?

Son(s): Self-control.

Father: Let's keep going.

Stop 3: Present them with a grip or a lanyard for the walking stick.

> Father: This grip represents self-control. Self-control helps us keep a firm grasp on what is important in life. It helps us to keep from dropping our faith. Is our journey complete?

Son(s): No.

Father: What do we need to add to our knowledge?

Son(s): Perseverance.

Father: Let's keep going.

Stop 4: Present them with a water bottle (up to this point, provide the water they need from your water bottle).

> Father: This water bottle represents perseverance. Water helps

THE JOURNEY OF CHIVALRY CEREMONY

us keep going; without it, we would die. Likewise, we will die spiritually without perseverance; we need it to keep going. Is our journey complete?

Son(s): No.

Father: What do we need to add to our perseverance?

Son(s): Godliness.

Father: Let's keep going.

Stop 5: Present them with a whistle.

Father: This whistle represents godliness. We must remember there is always someone else to whom we can call in times of need, and we need to serve Him and treat others as He would treat them. Is our journey complete?

Son(s): No.

Father: What do we need to add to our virtue?

Son(s): Brotherly kindness.

Father: Let's keep going.

Stop 6: Present them with a rope.

Father: This rope represents brotherly kindness. We can extend it to others to help them up if they have fallen, or use it to help them over difficult obstacles. Is our journey complete?

Son(s): No.

Father: What do we need to add to our brotherly kindness?

Son(s): Love.

Father: Let's keep going.

Stop 7: Present them with a flashlight.

Father: This flashlight represents the love we need to have for others. With it, you can help others out of the darkness and point the way towards God. It is a love that does not discriminate; everyone who sees the light benefits from it. So, everyone who comes around us should benefit from our love. Is our journey complete?

Son(s): No.

Father: Let's finish the journey.

Final Stop: Ideally, have the rest of your family and anyone else you want to include waiting with refreshments.

Father: This journey was difficult, and I'm proud of you for completing it. This journey, however, is just the start of another journey, one you will be on for the rest of your lives. You will need each of the items you picked up along the way to complete it successfully. Never forget to take faith, virtue, knowledge, self-control, perseverance, godliness, brotherly kindness, and love along with you. If these are yours and are increasing, you will be a useful and successful servant of our King.

End with a prayer: "Heavenly Father, the source of true knowledge, thank You for showing us the way we ought to live and for the times my son(s) and I have had to study these principles. Help us to walk in Your ways. Help us to be diligent and steadfast to follow these ideals of chivalry You have taught us. Help us to never give up and to complete the journey You have set before us. In the name of Jesus, amen."

LESSON 19

The Armor of God

INSTRUCTION

AMONG a knight's most treasured possessions are his weapons and armor. They are the tools that equipped him to fight and survive in battle. Knights are known for and recognized by their armor. Even in our minds today, the difference between a knight and an ordinary swordsman is the kind of armor he is wearing. Without the armor, we just see some guy with a sword.

Armor is protection. Soldiers engaged in war face enemies who wish to do them harm—thus the need for protection. Like them, we also have an enemy who wishes to do us harm. In Ephesians 6:12, the apostle Paul describes an epic struggle against the forces of evil. This is a not a battle against flesh and blood (i.e., it is not against people). Our enemy may work through people urging them to persecute us or tempt us off the path of righteousness, but no matter what a person does to us, they are not our real enemy. They are our mission, those to whom we must reach out. Paul tells us our true enemy is the spiritual forces of wickedness, an enemy that we cannot see with our eyes but who is very real. If we are to have any hope of standing firm in this battle, we must arm ourselves just as the knights in times past.

Knights could receive their armor in different ways. Some armor might be won in tournaments. Some armor might be handed down from father to son. Some would be provided armor by the knight they served as squires. The armor that we must take up, however, is provided by our King. We have the armor of God available to us, and there is no greater armor (cf. Ephesians 6:10-13).

It is called the armor of God because it belongs to Him. God Himself wears and uses this armor. In Isaiah 59:15-20, we see God using some of this armor. He has put on a breastplate of righteousness to deal with Israel's wickedness. He has also put the helmet of salvation on His head—ultimately His purpose is not to punish but to save His people. God is frequently described as one who protects His people as with a shield (cf. Genesis 15:1; Psalm 91:4; Proverbs 2:7; 30:5). Also, Isaiah prophesies that Jesus would gird His waist with the truth (Isaiah 11:5), His mouth would be like a sharp sword (Isaiah 49:2), and His feet would bring the good news of redemption and peace (Isaiah 52:7). These are similar to the armor of God Paul tells us to take up in Ephesians 6:14-17. God has taken up armor, and now it is time for us to take up this armor as well.

In days gone by, a knight would go to a blacksmith to have his armor fitted to him. The armor of God is different, though. To wear this armor, we must mold our lives to fit it. The next series of lessons will help us to take up the armor of God and fight the battle against wickedness. Are you ready to take up the armor of God? Review the contract you signed on the first day of training. Then sing "Soldiers of Christ Arise."

DAILY DRILLS

Aim at reviewing the parts of the armor of God with your son(s) once at day (maybe at night as they are going to bed).

>Father: "The belt of…"
>Son(s): "Truth!"
>
>Father: "The breastplate of…."
>Son(s): "Righteousness!"
>
>Father: "Feet shod with the…"
>Son(s): "Gospel of peace!"

THE ARMOR OF GOD

Father: "The shield of…"
Son(s): "Faith!"

Father: "The helmet of…"
Son(s): "Salvation!"

Father: "The sword of the…"
Son(s): "Spirit!

Father: "Which is…"
Son(s): "The Word of God!"

LESSON 20

The Belt of Truth

INSTRUCTION

A belt may not seem like an exciting piece of equipment, but it is an important one. After all, the belt is where the knight's sword would hang, and all of the plates of his armor are held together by a series of small belts and buckles. A knight could not arm himself without these belts. Likewise, we have an important belt we must put on if we are going to arm ourselves. In Ephesians 6:14, Paul tells us to: "Stand therefore, having girded your waist with truth." The enemy will try to deceive us with trickery and lies (cf. Ephesians 4:14-15; 6:11). We need truth to stand against our foe. Nothing else will do—not mere sincerity or desire. You may sincerely believe a lie and want it to be true, but that will not change the fact that it is a lie. Truth is important. Without truth, we will be defenseless before our enemy and his deceptions. We must put on the belt of truth to stand firm in the Lord.

However the belt of truth isn't a belt that is merely worn; this is a belt we are "to gird." *Girding* refers to a practice in the first century by which a person would prepare himself for action. This truth we are to gird ourselves with comes from Jesus (Ephesians 4:17-21). It cannot be found in the world or its ways; they have only darkness and ignorance. The truth is only found through learning about Jesus and His ways recorded for us in the Bible. Reading, studying, memorizing, and knowing the Word of God will protect you from the lies the enemy seeks to implant in your mind. Even these are not enough, however; truth must be put into practice. It must be lived (Ephesians 4:21-24; 5:9-10) and spoken (Ephesians 4:15, 25, 29). Only through studying, living, and speaking truth can we gird ourselves with the belt of truth and equip ourselves to fight.

CHAMPION OF THE TRUTH

Our champion of the truth is a prophet by the name of Micaiah. In 1 Kings 22, Ahab the king of Israel and Jehoshaphat the king of Judah are trying to determine what God thinks about them going up to fight against the king of Aram. Ahab gathers 400 prophets who say: "Sure, go to war, God will give you victory" (22:6, paraphrased). These prophets, however, are not from the Lord, and Jehoshaphat isn't satisfied (22:7). Here is where our champion enters. Ahab knows about Micaiah but doesn't like him because he never tells Ahab what he wants to hear—Ahab doesn't like hearing the truth (22:8). In verse 13, a messenger is sent to summon Micaiah and instructs him to say what all the other prophets have agreed to speak. Micaiah, however, says, "As the Lord lives, whatever the Lord says to me, that I will speak" (1 Kings 22:14). Micaiah is true to his word and reveals that Ahab will die if they go up to the battle and that all the other prophets have a deceiving spirit in them (1 Kings 22:17, 22-23). The chief of the lying prophets then strikes Micaiah on the cheek (22:24) and Ahab has Micaiah tossed into prison and instructs him to be fed sparingly (22:26-27). Although things seem bad for Micaiah, truth does win out. Ahab dies just as Micaiah predicted (22:34-35). Micaiah is one who speaks the truth when everyone around him is lying and pressuring him to lie. He speaks the truth even when it would cause him to suffer. We need to have his dedication to the truth.

STRATEGY

- How does truth protect us?
- What is the difference between truth and opinion?
- Why should we tell the truth?

THE BELT OF TRUTH

- What does lying do to our hearts?

- Are there lies you have told that you need to confess?

QUEST: LISTENING TO THE VOICE OF TRUTH

Set up an obstacle course and blindfold your son(s). Guide him through the obstacle course by giving him only vocal instructions. The point: Just as he could only avoid the obstacles by listening to your voice, only by living according to the truth of God's Word can we avoid the pitfalls of this life. God's Word will even help us to avoid dangers we cannot see.

Now, blindfold yourself and give you son a chance to guide you through the course. The point: Only by telling the truth can you help others; lying will only end up harming others and keeping them from the goal.

TO TRAIN UP A KNIGHT

LESSON 21

The Breastplate of Righteousness

INSTRUCTION

THE breastplate is that which protects the chest and main body of the knight. In history, the full plate armor of the knights began to be abandoned piece by piece as firearms made them obsolete. The breastplate, however, was one of the last pieces to go. You can survive without an arm or a leg, but you cannot survive without your heart or lungs or with a big gaping hole in your gut. Righteousness is like a breastplate to a servant of God. There are many flaws in our character we will need to work on and heal from, but without righteousness we are hypocrites, and that is deadly. Thus, Paul tells us to "put on the breastplate of righteousness" (Ephesians 6:4). Righteousness in this sense is the desire to do everything right and good as God would want us to do. This kind of lifestyle enables you to stand firm even against those who are opposed to such living because you know you are right with your King and that is all that really matters.

In Ephesians 4:20-24, Paul gives us instructions regarding taking up a life of righteousness. Notice the progression Paul describes: 1) hear the truth (4:20-21), 2) lay aside wickedness (4:22), 3) be renewed in your mind (4:23), 4) put on a new self which in the likeness of God has been created in righteousness and holiness (4:24). Notice how this part of the armor builds upon the belt of truth. As we hear the truth and put it into practice, we take up the breastplate of righteousness as well. Paul goes one to give several examples of this process in Ephesians 4:25–5:21. Notice a few: we turn from falsehood to truth (4:25), we turn from anger to control (4:26-27), and we turn from bitterness to forgiveness (4:30-32). In Ephesians 5:22–6:9, Paul shows what righteousness looks like in various relationships. Notice how he describes the father-child relationship in Ephesians 6:3-4. A father-child relationship displays righteousness when the father brings the child up in the training and admonition of the Lord and when the child listens and obeys his or her parents.

CHAMPION OF RIGHTEOUSNESS

Our champion of righteousness is the apostle Paul. In Acts 21–26, Paul is in a series of trials in defense of his life, ministry, and actions. Since Paul lived a righteous life, he is able to make statements like these in his defense: "Men and brethren, I have lived in all good conscience before God until this day" (Acts 23:1). "They neither found me in the temple disputing with anyone nor inciting the crowd, either in the synagogues or in the city. Nor can they prove the things of which they now accuse me" (Acts 24:12-13). "Let those who are here themselves say if they found any wrongdoing in me while I stood before the council (Acts 24:20). "Neither against the law of the Jews, nor against the temple, nor against Caesar have I offended in anything at all" (Acts 25:8). "To the Jews I have done no wrong, as you very well know. For if I am an offender, or have committed anything deserving of death, I do not object to dying; but if there is nothing in these things of which these men accuse me, no one can deliver me to them. I appeal to Caesar" (Acts 25:10-11). Twice during these trials, it is recorded that Paul has not done anything worthy of death or imprisonment (25:25; 26:30-32). Even better however, Paul is able to share the Gospel with the powerful and influential. Although we cannot be sure of the tone in which this statement is delivered, one of them says: "You almost persuade me to become a Christian" (Acts 26:28). We see in the life of Paul how righteous living protects a person and increases their influence when teaching others about God.

THE BREASTPLATE OF RIGHTEOUSNESS

STRATEGY

- How can righteousness protect us?
- Who sets the standards for what is righteous?
- How do we learn these standards?
- What should we do if something is unrighteous?

QUEST: FLEE FROM UNRIGHTEOUSNESS

Establish a home base (a blanket or a chair or something to which your son can run) and put your son at a reasonable distance between you and the base. You are "Mr. Conscience." To play, have your son ask: "What are you thinking, Mr. Conscience?" If you say something that is good and righteous (e.g., "I'm thinking about prayer," "I'm thinking about helping someone," etc.), nothing happens and your son asks the question again. If you say something that is unrighteous (e.g., "I'm thinking about lying," "I'm thinking about being a bully," etc.), they run towards home while you try to tag them before they get there.

TO TRAIN UP A KNIGHT

LESSON 22

Feet Prepared by the Gospel

INSTRUCTION

YOU aren't really ready until you have your shoes on. We need shoes to protect our feet, and they are required for many of the places we go. Likewise, shoes are required for us to be ready for the spiritual war. In Ephesians 6:15, Paul describes the next part of the armor of God as "having shod your feet with the preparation of the Gospel of peace." The Gospel prepares us for spiritual battle because it provides peace. Being prepared indicates "an intellectual readiness, ability, or resolution of mind." What prepares our minds for actions and serving God is the knowledge of peace that comes from obeying the Gospel. The Gospel provides peace between God and man (Ephesians 2:13-18). It also creates a bond among other servants of God that we strive to maintain (Ephesians 4:1-6) and work together with them for the sake of the Kingdom (Ephesians 4:7-16).

There is a great peace that fills our lives when we walk in such a worthy manner. We no longer have to worry about what others think about us or say about us because we can be confident we are at peace with God. No matter what others try to do to us or say about us, we know we have a solid relationship with God and we are where we need to be. Also, much of the stress and worry of this life comes from the things of this world (getting them and keeping them) and from pain. The Gospel, however, shows us we are heading towards something better—Heaven. Thus, the things of this world are of little concern, and our lives will be filled with peace. This leads to a life of joy and a desire to help others experience that joy. Notice again how the parts of the armor are working together. Hearing and applying truth leads us to take up righteous living, and righteous living leads to peace with God and ourselves.

CHAMPION OF PEACEFULNESS

Our champion of peacefulness is Stephen. Stephen is known as the first recorded person to be martyred for the faith. In Acts 6, Stephen begins to teach others about Christ. He reasons with them powerfully. Some, not liking this, accuse him of blasphemy. In Acts 7, Stephen is given the opportunity to speak in defense of himself. Instead of backing off or apologizing, Stephen gives them a sermon in which He recounts God's work outside of Israel and the unfaithfulness of Israel. Then, he tells them they are just like those who had rejected God in the past. They are so angry that they drag Stephen outside the town and begin to stone him. Here is the really amazing part—while they are stoning Stephen, Stephen is looking upward toward Heaven and praying to forgive the people who are brutally killing him. How is he able to do this? He has confidence that comes from knowing he is right with God. His feet are shod with the preparation that comes from the Gospel of peace. The accusations don't matter to him because he knows he is right with God. The stoning doesn't bother him because he knows he is headed somewhere better. This enables him to rise above the worries and problems of this life and act as Christ would. Let us do the same.

STRATEGY

- Do you feel at peace with yourself? Why or why not?
- Do you feel at peace with God? Why or why not?
- How do you feel when others make fun of you?

QUEST: THE WALK OF CONFIDENCE

Find a place that is just a little uncomfortable—but not dangerous so—to walk barefoot (like a hot sidewalk or a gravel driveway). Have your son stand barefoot as long as he can without shifting his feet. Then, have him put on his shoes and try standing again. The first time is like going through life without the peace of the Gospel. You have a hard time standing your ground because of the discomfort. The discomfort comes from others or ourselves accusing us and pointing out our weaknesses. The second time we know we have protection, and we aren't worried about pain or discomfort; we are at peace. The discomfort is gone, and we can stand our ground. This is what it is like when you are right with God and sure about your eternal destination.

LESSON 23

The Shield of Faith

INSTRUCTION

A knight is one who fights wholeheartedly in battle. He puts his all into the fight knowing his cause is just and his leader is honest. A warrior without these convictions opens himself to attack. Doubts about the commands and ability of his leader cause him to hesitate and make him vulnerable on the field. We must not be such warriors; we must be knights. It is faith that will make the difference. As Paul commands us to take up the armor of God, he says: "Above all, taking the shield of faith with which you will be able to quench all the fiery darts of the wicked one" (Ephesians 6:16). We must have no doubts about the promises and commands of God. We must have confidence in the message of truth (cf. Ephesians 1:13). We must firmly believe there is a reward waiting in Heaven, and we must move in that direction. Such faith becomes a shield that protects us and keeps us moving in the right direction.

Satan has many schemes and tactics he will use against us. He will lie and he will torment us. No matter what attack Satan launches at us, however, faith will carry us through. If he encourages us to engage in foolishness, faith will help us see wisdom and understand the will of God (Ephesians 1:15-17). If he tries to discourage us, faith lifts us up so that we may see hope (Ephesians 1:18). If he tells us serving God isn't worth it, faith reminds us of the riches of our inheritance (Ephesians 1:18b). If he tries to convince us that we are too weak and unable to stand, faith looks to the great and awesome God who is infinitely more powerful than Satan (Ephesians 1:19-21). All of this is done by faith. When we have strong faith, we will have a strong relationship with the Lord and be able to stand against the lies of Satan.

CHAMPION OF FAITH

Our champion of faith is also known as "the father of the faithful." Abraham is one who is given several promises from God that require great belief (cf. Genesis 12:1-3). God tells Abraham that He would make a great nation out of him. Abraham and Sarah, however, seem incapable of having children. Nevertheless, Abraham hopes against hope. Although Abraham has many reasons not to believe this promise, he never wavers in regards to the promises of God (Romans 4:17-20). Abraham's faith is not in vain; God is true to His promise (Genesis 21:1-3). Abraham's faith, however, is tested in many other ways. Perhaps the greatest test of Abraham's faith is when God's telling him to sacrifice this child of promise upon an altar to God (Genesis 22:1-2). Abraham does not hesitate or waver in unbelief (Genesis 22:3-4). He does not question his God. He knows Isaac is the child of promise and that somehow both he and Isaac would come down from that mountain (Genesis 22:5), even if God has to raise Isaac from the dead (Hebrews 11:17-19). There are many more promises that Abraham believes in even though he would not see them in his lifetime. He is told his descendants would inherit the land of Israel, but not for over 400 years (Genesis 15:13-16). He is told that "in his seed" all the nations of the earth would be blessed—a promise that would not be fulfilled until Jesus comes almost 2,000 years later (cf. Galatians 3:16). In addition to all of these promises, Abraham is searching for an even greater promise—a heavenly country with a city prepared by God (Hebrews 11:10, 13-16). If we have such a faith as Abraham's, we will be able to stand firm in the faith no matter what obstacles we may encounter.

THE SHIELD OF FAITH

STRATEGY

- Do you follow God's Word even when you think a different way may be better?

- Are you ready to tell the truth even when it may mean you are punished for something you have done wrong?

- Are you ready to live righteously even when others may make fun of you?

- Are you concerned that following God's Word may not be right for you?

QUEST: TRUST FALL

Have your son stand with his back to you and his arms folded against his chest. Instruct him to fall backward when you say "Now." Try it several times until he can confidently fall backward, and then have him stand on a stable elevated surface (a step, a porch, or something of this nature) again. At first, this may be difficult, but the more trust is exercised and rewarded, the more trust grows. Even though he cannot see you, he knows you are there and will catch him. The same happens when we believe God's Word and follow it even through trials. God's Word bears fruit, and our faith becomes perfected (cf. James 1:2-4).

LESSON 24

The Helmet of Salvation

INSTRUCTION

THE head must be protected at all costs. Even a glancing blow to the head could leave a knight dazed and confused, unsure of what to do, and more direct hits would deal death. So, a knight puts on his helmet to protect himself. Like the other parts of our armor, this helmet belongs to God. We see God taking up this helmet in Isaiah 19:15-17 and 20. At this point in history, Israel has become so corrupt that God has clothed Himself to intercede. Not only has He put on a breastplate of righteousness, clothed Himself with vengeance and wrapped Himself in a mantle of zeal, but He has also put salvation on His head. Salvation is the ultimate purpose, the goal of all of His actions. Not His salvation, of course, but ours (cf. 1 Timothy 2:3-4; 2 Peter 3:9). Now, we are instructed to take up God's purpose of salvation so that we might stand strong against the forces of evil. This purpose provides a focus—a way of thinking that will guide our lives.

For us, there are two goals we need to have to put on the helmet of salvation. The first goal is our salvation—making it to Heaven. The second goal is the salvation of others—to bring as many with us as possible. These goals help to focus our lives on what is truly important and cut out that which will get in the way. They keep us from wandering around aimlessly, dazed and confused. These goals will not be achieved by accident or by sitting back and doing nothing. They require us to become deeply involved in serving the King and His Kingdom—studying His Word, attending worship services and Bible studies, inviting others to Bible study. Those who will exert the effort will find themselves standing securely in the battle against the forces of wickedness.

CHAMPION OF SALVATION

While many of the faithful men and women of the Bible armed themselves with the helmet of salvation, the apostle Paul especially stands out. Some historians credit Paul's work with the rapid spread of Christianity in the first few centuries A.D. He is so devoted to the Gospel and teaching others that tradition records he converts the men that are sent to execute him. In Corinthians 9:19-23, Paul expresses his desire to do all things for the sake of the Gospel so that he can win as many as possible and share in the blessings of the Gospel. He is willing to be a slave, willing to conform himself to laws and customs he does not have to follow, and willing to put himself in unfamiliar and uncomfortable situations. Apart from disobeying God's commands, he would do whatever is necessary to save souls. He doesn't stop there however. Paul goes on in 1 Corinthians 9:24-27 to explain how he disciplines himself so that he would not lose his salvation. To this purpose Paul takes aim—he does not run without purpose or beat the air. He disciplines himself—he beats his body into submission to accomplish his goals and live as a Christian. Paul's fear of losing his salvation helps him to discipline himself and make sure he is not hindering the Gospel. We must follow Paul's example in selflessly reaching out to others for the sake of the Gospel and dedicating ourselves to living it.

STRATEGY

- What is the purpose of your life?
- What goals do you have in life? What would you like to do?
- Are these goals in line with the purpose of God? Will they

THE HELMET OF SALVATION

take you further from the purpose of God? Or neither?

- What can you do to help others follow God's Word?

QUEST: HITTING THE MARK

Find a target or two and something to throw and shoot at them (darts and a dartboard would work great, or maybe a paper target and spitballs). Do two rounds—the first just shoot randomly without aiming at the bullseye, the second time carefully aim at the bullseye. The first round should be rather scattered with most missing the mark; the second should be grouped closer together and closer to the bullseye. The difference is keeping your eye on the goal. Reaching our goal of being with God will not happen unless we keep our eyes on the prize.

TO TRAIN UP A KNIGHT

LESSON 25

The Sword of the Spirit

INSTRUCTION

NO matter how good a knight might be at defending himself, he couldn't win a battle without striking back. If the knight is hesitant to strike or is afraid to open himself up by attacking, he would never gain ground. It is the same with our spiritual struggle described in Ephesians 6:10-13. Notice the word translated "withstand" or "resist" in verse 13. This word means "to stand against"[1] and contains the concept not just of standing your ground but of opposing your foe. Our armor helps us to stand our ground, but we are given more than armor. We are given a weapon with which we can fight back—the sword of the Spirit. This sword is the Scriptures the Holy Spirit has inspired so that we will know the will of God and be thoroughly equipped for every good work (cf. Ephesians 3:4-5; 2 Timothy 3:16-17; 2 Peter 1:19-21). It is time for us to take up this sword and consider how we can use this sword in our fight against evil.

To use a sword well, we have to be familiar with it—to know its weight, its balance, and its length. The sword must feel comfortable in our hands like it is a natural extension of ourselves. This requires study and practice. If we are to take up the sword of the Spirit, we must put in the time and effort required to study and know the Word. Then, we must begin to practice what we learn in our lives. We don't stop there, however. We go on to tell others what we have learned to help them follow God's will (cf. Ezra 7:10). When we faithfully use the sword of the Spirit in this way, it sets others free from Satan's influence and

---

[1] Zodhiates, Spiros, *The Complete Word Study Dictionary: New Testament* (Chattanooga, TN: AMG Publishers, 2000) n. pag.

destroys his work.

CHAMPION OF SWORDSMANSHIP

The apostle Peter is our champion of swordsmanship. When we begin to learn about Peter in the Gospels, we see him as a man who wavers between saying the exactly right thing and sticking his foot in his mouth; he goes through extremes from showing great faith to denying Jesus. In Acts 2, however, Peter receives the Holy Spirit. From this point on, Peter begins to show greater maturity. On that day, he stands with the other apostles and proclaims the Gospel for the first time (Acts 2:14-36). Out of the 23 verses of his lesson, 12 of them are direct quotes from the Scriptures. He uses the Word of God as evidence and proof of what he is saying. He proclaims the Word of God accurately, encouraging others to repent and be baptized (Acts 2:38). He makes it known that salvation is possible only in Jesus Christ (Acts 4:11). When men object to his proclamation of the Gospel, he knows he has to obey God and keep speaking what God has told him (cf. Acts 4:19-20; 5:29-32). Later, Peter would write, "If anyone speaks, let him speak as the oracles of God. If anyone ministers, let him do it as with the ability which God supplies, that in all things God may be glorified through Jesus Christ, to whom belong the glory and the dominion forever and ever. Amen" (1 Peter 4:11).

STRATEGY

- How well do you know the Bible?
- What can you do to learn more about God's Word?
- What have you learned that you have a hard time following?
- What are ways you can help others with God's Word?

THE SWORD OF THE SPIRIT

QUEST: DEFEATING UNGODLINESS

You will need a least ten balloons and something pointy and sword-like that can pop the balloons (e.g., a letter opener, a skewer, a needle, a push pin, or a pocket knife if your son can handle it safely). Blow up the ten balloons. Then label five of them *Lies*, *Temptation*, *False Doctrine*, *Sin*, and *Foolishness*. Label the other five *Teach*, *Correct*, *Train*, *Encourage*, and *Learn*. Then, tape the balloons to a wall, or, for more of a challenge, hang them by a string from the ceiling. Give your son the letter opener (or whatever) and tell him it is the sword of the Spirit and he needs to use it to pop all the things the sword can help us defeat and leave the things it helps us to do.

TO TRAIN UP A KNIGHT

LESSON 26

The Prayers of the Saints

INSTRUCTION

NO matter how well armed, skilled, or brave a knight might be, a good knight knows he needs help. Immediately after describing the armor of God, Paul tells us we need to be constantly praying (Ephesians 6:17-20). In hard times when we are struggling, we need to pray to God. When everything is going great, we need to pray to God so that we will be alert and on guard. Our enemy loves it when we become careless and stop paying attention. We must be diligent so that he cannot gain the upper hand. If we are wearing our armor, we are on the alert, and we are asking our God for help, there is no way our enemy can overcome us.

Prayer is more than just calling out for help and paying attention, however; it is one way we can be actively engaged in battle. Paul encourages us to be actively praying for our comrades in arms. We should be watching out and praying for each other, not just ourselves. We must think of ourselves more like a united army than individuals in this war. We show this by praying for one another and especially when we know someone is struggling or in need. Also, we pray for our cause. We pray for the Kingdom of Heaven (Matthew 6:9-10) and that its workers will find open doors and be able to make the message clear (Colossians 4:2-4). Always remember: "The effective, fervent prayer of a righteous man avails much" (James 5:16b).

CHAMPION

Our champion of prayer is a man by the name of Nehemiah.

TO TRAIN UP A KNIGHT

Nehemiah lives during the period of Israel's return from captivity, but he is still in the land of captivity. Nevertheless, he cares deeply for his homeland. In Nehemiah 1:1-3, he finds out that his people are in distress, and Jerusalem's walls are still broken down. He is deeply grieved about the situation and then he takes action—he begins to pray (Nehemiah 1:4-11). Nehemiah is very open and honest in his prayer to God. He knows that Israel has sinned and confesses this to God. He also knows if they repent that God would help them once again. He expresses this hope and this desire to God. Nehemiah does not just pray once, though; he prays patiently and persistently for 3 ½ to 5 months before God answers his prayer.

Nehemiah goes on to be one of Israel's greatest and most successful leaders, and it all starts with prayer. He humbles himself and submits to God's will and God's solution. We need to become prayer warriors like Nehemiah and put our trust in God's ways, not our own.

STRATEGY

- How often do you pray?
- At what times/occasions should we pray?
- How do you feel about your prayer life?
- Do you feel like God is listening to your prayers?

QUEST: THE ACTS OF PRAYER

Make a prayer list with your son(s). Divide your prayer list into four areas using the ACTS model of prayer:

- **A**doration (cf. 1 Chronicles 29:10-13)
- **C**onfession (cf. Psalm 51)

- **T**hanksgiving (cf. John 11:41-42)
- **S**upplication (cf. 1 Thessalonians 3:11-13)

Then pray together.

TO TRAIN UP A KNIGHT

The Armor of God Ceremony

THIS final ceremony is an opportunity to encourage them to stand strong in God's ways. Just as the other ceremonies, how elaborate or detailed you make this one is up to you. However, try to make this one larger and more involved than the others. You might include the whole family and find a role for your wife in the ceremony. Consider having a special dinner or feast for the setting of this ceremony.

SAMPLE CEREMONY:

In a private room before the meal, have a one-hour vigil with your son(s) by spending five minutes on each of the areas of prayer and contemplation listed below. It will be helpful to read through this and prepare prayer lists. Take turns in each of these until your time is up. (e.g., you pray praising God, and then your son does, and then another son or you pray again).

1. Wait—Take five minutes to focus on what you are about to do.

2. Praise—Try to just praise God and His nature.

3. Confession—Acknowledge your weaknesses and sins that cause you to fall short of God's glory.

4. Read the Word—Suggested texts:

    Matthew 5:2-12
    2 Peter 1:2-11
    Ephesians 6:10-18
    1 Timothy 6:11-16
    Joshua 1:6-9
    Jeremiah 1:4-10

> 1 Kings 2:1-4

5. Intercession—This is time spent praying for the physical and spiritual needs of others (a prayer list will come in handy).

6. Petition—Time spent praying for our own physical and spiritual needs (a prayer list might be helpful here, too).

7. Pray the Word—Praying His Word assures us we are praying His will.

   > Psalm 144
   > Psalm 25
   > Psalm 27

8. Thanksgiving—This is our gift to God (cf. Philippians 4:6).

9. Singing—These songs come straight from the heart (cf. Psalm 110:2).

   > "Soldiers of Christ Arise"
   > "Onward Christian Soldiers"
   > "I'm a Hard Fighting Soldier"
   > "The Battle Belongs to the Lord"

10. Meditate—Ponder the meaning of the conversation you have just had (cf. Joshua 1:8).

11. Plan—Decide how you are going to put into practice what you have learned (cf. Proverbs 16:9).

12. End by praising God again.

[After the one hour vigil, move to the feast room]

> Father: In Ephesians 6:10-17, Paul commands us to take up the armor of God. Let us remember the parts:

THE ARMOR OF GOD CEREMONY

Father: "The belt of…"
Son(s): "Truth."

Father: "The breastplate of…"
Son(s): "Righteousness."

Father: "Feet shod with…"
Son(s): "The Gospel of peace."

Father: "The shield of…"
Son(s): "Faith."

Father: The helmet of…"
Son(s): "Salvation."

Father: "The sword of…"
Son(s): "The Spirit."

Father: "Which is…"
Son(s): "The Word of God."

Father: Remember—all these parts of the armor of God work together. It is by hearing and applying the truth that we can take up righteous living, and righteous living leads to peace with God and ourselves. Peace with God and ourselves leads to faith; faith leads to a desire to save others. A desire to save others leads us to use the sword of the Spirit and to pray. Only with all of these working together can we stand strong in our battle and resist the evil one.

I always enjoy the times we have come together to study God's armor. I want to give you a small gift to help you remember the lessons you have learned and the principles you will need to stand firm. [There are pins easily found with the armor of God on them and even "real" swords that can be found on Amazon for around $20. Have their mother put the pins or the sword on them.]

> Mother: (Son's name), I love you. Be strong in the Lord and in the strength of His might. Put on the full armor of God.

End with a prayer: "Heavenly Father and source of our strength and our refuge in times of trouble, thank You for the armor You have provided for us and thank You for the times my son(s) and I have had to study God's Word together. Thank You for this occasion in my son's life to celebrate their desire to serve You. Help us to take up Your armor and stand strong in Your might. In the name of Jesus, amen."

Go celebrate with a feast.

www.ingramcontent.com/pod-product-compliance
Lightning Source LLC
Chambersburg PA
CBHW070630300426
44113CB00010B/1722